The Firebugs

The Firebugs

A MORALITY WITHOUT A MORAL

A PLAY BY

MAX FRISCH

TRANSLATED BY

MICHAEL BULLOCK

A DRAMABOOK

ⓦ Hill and Wang · New York

Translation copyright © 1962 by Michael Bullock
Originally published in German as *Herr Biedermann und die Brandstifter*
Copyright © 1958 by Suhrkamp Verlag, Frankfurt am Main
All rights reserved
Published in Canada by HarperCollins*CanadaLtd*
This English translation originally published as
The Fire Raisers by Methuen London Ltd in 1962
First American edition, 1985
Library of Congress catalog card number: 85-61022

Fifth printing, 1993

CHARACTERS

GOTTLIEB BIEDERMANN
BABETTE, *his wife*
ANNA, *a maidservant*
SEPP SCHMITZ, *a wrestler*
WILLI EISENRING, *a waiter*
A POLICEMAN
A PH.D.
MRS. KNECHTLING
THE CHORUS OF FIREMEN

SCENE: A simultaneous setting, showing the living room and
        the attic of BIEDERMANN'S house
TIME: Now

The stage is dark, then a match flares, revealing the face of Herr Biedermann, who is lighting a cigar. As it grows lighter he looks around him. He is surrounded by firemen in helmets.

BIEDERMANN One can't even light a cigar nowadays without thinking of fire! ... It's revolting –
Biedermann hides the smoking cigar and withdraws, whereupon the Fire Brigade steps forward in the manner of a classical Greek chorus. A tower-clock strikes the quarter.

CHORUS Good people of our city, see
Us, its guardians,
Looking,
Listening,
Full of good will towards the well-intentioned citizen –

CHORUS LEADER Who, after all, pays our wages.

CHORUS Splendidly equipped
We prowl around your house,
At once alert and free from suspicion.

CHORUS LEADER Sometimes, too, we sit down,
But without sleeping, tirelessly

CHORUS Looking,
Listening,
For that which is concealed
To be revealed,
Before it is too late
To put out
The first few flickers
Threatening fire.
A tower-clock strikes the half.

CHORUS LEADER Many things may start a fire,
But not every fire that starts
Is the work of inexorable
Fate.

CHORUS Other things, called Fate to prevent you
From asking how they happened,
Monstrous events,
Even the total destruction of a city,
Are mischief.

CHORUS LEADER Human,

CHORUS All too human

CHORUS LEADER Mischief that wipes out
Our mortal fellow citizens.
A tower-clock strikes the three-quarters.

CHORUS Much can be avoided
By common sense.

CHORUS LEADER In very truth:

CHORUS It is unworthy of God,
Unworthy of man,
To call a stupidity Fate
Simply because it has happened.
The man who acts so
No longer deserves the name,
No longer deserves God's earth,
Inexhaustible, fruitful and kind,
Nor the air that he breathes,
Nor the sun.
Bestow not the name of Fate
Upon man's mistakes,
Even the worst,
Beyond our power to put out!
The tower-clock strikes the hour.

CHORUS LEADER Our watch has begun.
The chorus sits down while the clock strikes nine.

I

ROOM

Gottlieb Biedermann is sitting in his room reading the newspaper and smoking a cigar. Anna, the maid, in a white apron, brings a bottle of wine.

ANNA Herr Biedermann?

No answer.

Herr Biedermann –

He folds up the newspaper.

BIEDERMANN They ought to be strung up. Haven't I always said
so? Another fire. And the same old story as I live
and breathe: another hawker who settles down in
the loft, a harmless hawker . . .

He takes the bottle.

They ought to be strung up!

He takes the corkscrew.

ANNA Herr Biedermann –

BIEDERMANN What is it?

ANNA He's still there.

BIEDERMANN Who?

ANNA The hawker who wants to speak to you.

BIEDERMANN I'm not at home!

ANNA That's what I told him, Herr Biedermann, an
hour ago. He says he knows you. I can't throw that
man out, Herr Biedermann, I simply can't.

BIEDERMANN Why not?

ANNA He's far too big and strong . . .

Biedermann draws the cork.

BIEDERMANN Tell him to come and see me in my office
tomorrow.

ANNA I have told him, Herr Biedermann, three times,
but he isn't interested.

BIEDERMANN Why not?

ANNA He doesn't want any hair tonic.

BIEDERMANN Then what does he want?

ANNA Humanity . . .

Biedermann sniffs at the cork.

BIEDERMANN Tell him I shall come and throw him out with
my own hands if he doesn't beat it immediately.

He carefully fills his Burgundy glass.

Humanity! . . .

He tastes the wine.

Tell him to wait out in the hall. I'll be there in a

minute. If he's selling something, tracts or razor blades, I'm not hard-hearted, but – I'm not hard-hearted, Anna, you know that! – but I'm not going to have anyone coming into the house. I've told you that a hundred times! Even if we had three beds free I wouldn't consider it. We know what that can lead to – nowadays . . .

Anna turns to go and sees that the stranger has just entered: an athlete, his clothes are reminiscent both of a jail and of a circus, his arms are tattooed, and he wears leather straps round his wrists. Anna creeps out. The stranger waits till Biedermann has sipped his wine and looks round.

SCHMITZ Good evening.

Biedermann drops his cigar with astonishment.

Your cigar, Herr Biedermann –

He picks up the cigar and gives it to Biedermann.

BIEDERMANN I say –

SCHMITZ Good evening!

BIEDERMANN What's the meaning of this? I expressly told the maid you were to wait out in the hall. What possessed you . . . I mean . . . without knocking . . .

SCHMITZ My name is Schmitz.

BIEDERMANN Without knocking.

SCHMITZ Joseph Schmitz.

Silence.

Good evening!

BIEDERMANN What do you want?

SCHMITZ There's nothing to worry about, Herr Biedermann: I'm not a hawker!

BIEDERMANN Then what are you?

SCHMITZ A wrestler by trade.

BIEDERMANN A wrestler?

SCHMITZ A heavy-weight.

BIEDERMANN I see.

SCHMITZ That's to say, I was.

BIEDERMANN And now?

SCHMITZ I'm out of work.

Pause.

Don't worry, Herr Biedermann, I'm not looking for work. On the contrary. I'm fed up with wrestling . . . I only came in because it's raining so hard outside.

Pause.

It's warmer in here.

Pause.

I hope I'm not disturbing you –

Pause.

BIEDERMANN Do you smoke?

He offers cigars.

SCHMITZ It's terrible to be as big as I am, Herr Biedermann. Everyone's afraid of me . . .

Biedermann gives him a light.

Thanks.

They stand smoking.

BIEDERMANN To come to the point, what do you want?

SCHMITZ My name is Schmitz.

BIEDERMANN So you said, well, how do you do?

SCHMITZ I'm homeless.

He holds the cigar under his nose and savours the aroma.

I'm homeless.

BIEDERMANN Would you like – a slice of bread?

SCHMITZ If that's all you've got . . .

BIEDERMANN Or a glass of wine?

SCHMITZ Bread and wine . . . But only if I'm not disturbing you, Herr Biedermann, only if I'm not disturbing you!

Biedermann goes to the door.

BIEDERMANN Anna!

Biedermann comes back.

SCHMITZ The maid told me Herr Biedermann was going to throw me out personally, but I couldn't believe you really meant it, Herr Biedermann . . .

Anna has entered.

BIEDERMANN Anna, bring a second glass.

ANNA Very good.

BIEDERMANN And some bread – yes.

SCHMITZ And if you don't mind, Fräulein, some butter.
And some cheese or cold meat or something. Only
don't put yourself out. A few pickled cucumbers,
a tomato or something, a little mustard – whatever you happen to have, Fräulein.

ANNA Very good.

SCHMITZ Only don't put yourself out!
Anna goes out.

BIEDERMANN You know me, the maid said.

SCHMITZ Of course, Herr Biedermann, of course.

BIEDERMANN Where from?

SCHMITZ Only from your best side, Herr Biedermann, only
from your best side. Yesterday evening in the
local – I know you didn't notice me in the corner
– everyone in there was delighted every time
you banged the table with your fist, Herr Biedermann.

BIEDERMANN What was I saying?

SCHMITZ Absolutely the right thing.
He smokes his cigar, then:
They ought to be strung up. All of them. The
quicker, the better. Strung up. All these
firebugs....
Biedermann offers Schmitz a chair.

BIEDERMANN Take a seat.
Schmitz sits down.

SCHMITZ Men like you, Herr Biedermann, that's what we
need!

BIEDERMANN Yes, no doubt, but –

SCHMITZ No buts, Herr Biedermann, no buts! You're one
of the Old Brigade, you still have a positive out-
look. That explains it.

BIEDERMANN No doubt –

SCHMITZ You still have civil courage.

BIEDERMANN No doubt –

SCHMITZ That explains it.

BIEDERMANN Explains what?

SCHMITZ You still have a conscience, everyone in the local could feel that, a real conscience.

BIEDERMANN Yes, yes, of course –

SCHMITZ Herr Biedermann, it's not of course at all. Not nowadays. In the circus where I wrestled, for example – and that's why the whole circus was burnt to the ground afterwards – our manager said to me: Take a running jump at yourself, Joe! – my name is Joseph, you know – take a running jump, he said, why should I have a conscience? Those were his very words. What I need to keep my beasts in order is a whip. Those were his very words. That's the kind of fellow he was. Conscience, he laughed. If anyone has a conscience it's generally a guilty one . . .
He smokes with enjoyment.
God rest his soul.

BIEDERMANN You mean he's dead?

SCHMITZ Burnt to death with the whole shoot.
A grandfather clock strikes nine.

BIEDERMANN I can't think what's keeping that girl!

SCHMITZ I'm in no hurry. –
The two men happen suddenly to look into each other's eyes. And you haven't a bed free in the house, Herr Biedermann, the maid has already told me –

BIEDERMANN Why do you laugh?

SCHMITZ Unfortunately there isn't a bed free! That's what they all say the moment they see a homeless person – and I don't even want a bed.

BIEDERMANN No?

SCHMITZ I'm used to sleeping on the floor, Herr Biedermann. My father was a charcoal burner. I'm used to it . . .
He smokes.
No buts, Herr Biedermann, no buts, I say! You aren't one of those who talk big in pubs because

they're scared stiff. I believe you. Unfortunately
there isn't a bed free – that's what they all say –
but you I believe, Herr Biedermann . . . Where
shall we end up if nobody believes anyone else
any more? That's what I always say, where shall
we end up? Everybody thinks everybody else is a
firebug, there's nothing but distrust in the
world. Don't you agree? The whole pub could feel
that, Herr Biedermann: you still believe in the
good in man and in yourself. Don't you agree?
You're the first person in this town who hasn't
simply treated me like an arsonist –

BIEDERMANN Here's an ash tray.

SCHMITZ Don't you agree?

He carefully taps the ash off his cigar.

Most people nowadays believe in the Fire Brigade
instead of in God.

BIEDERMANN What do you mean by that?

SCHMITZ The truth.

Anna brings a tray.

ANNA We haven't any cold meat.

SCHMITZ That'll do, Fräulein, that'll do – except that you've
forgotten the mustard.

ANNA Sorry!

Anna goes out.

BIEDERMANN Tuck in! –

Biedermann fills the glasses.

SCHMITZ You don't get this kind of reception everywhere,
Herr Biedermann. I've had some nasty experi-
ences, I can tell you. No sooner is a fellow like
me across the threshold – a man without a tie,
homeless and hungry – than they say, sit down,
and ring the police behind my back. What do
you think of that? I ask for a roof over my head,
nothing more, an honest wrestler who has been
wrestling all his life; some gentleman who has
never wrestled comes along and takes me by the
collar – What's the idea? I ask and I merely turn

round, just to have a look at him, and already his
shoulder's broken.

He takes the glass:

Cheers!

They drink and Schmitz starts eating.

BIEDERMANN Well, you know how things are these days. You
can't open a newspaper without reading of another
case of arson! And it's always the same story: a
hawker asks for shelter and next morning the
house goes up in flames . . . I simply mean I can
understand people being a bit distrustful.

He picks up his newspaper.

Here, look at this!

*He puts the open newspaper down beside Schmitz's
plate.*

SCHMITZ I've seen it.

BIEDERMANN A whole district.

He stands up to show Schmitz.

Here, read this!

Schmitz eats and reads and drinks.

SCHMITZ Beaujolais?

BIEDERMANN Yes.

SCHMITZ It would have been better with the chill off . . .

He reads across his plate:

' – It seems that the fire was planned and started
in the same manner as last time.'

They eye one another.

BIEDERMANN Isn't it incredible?

Schmitz puts the newspaper away.

SCHMITZ That's why I don't read the newspapers any
more.

BIEDERMANN How do you mean?

SCHMITZ Because it's always the same.

BIEDERMANN Yes, yes, of course, but – that's no solution, just
not reading the newspaper; I mean you have to
know what lies in store for you.

SCHMITZ Why?

BIEDERMANN Well, you just have to.

SCHMITZ It will come, Herr Biedermann, it will come.
He sniffs the sausage.
The judgment of God.
He cuts himself a slice of sausage.

BIEDERMANN Do you think so?
Anna brings the mustard.

SCHMITZ Thank you, Fräulein, thank you.
Is there anything else?

SCHMITZ Not today.
Anna remains by the door.
There's nothing I like better than mustard, you
know.
He squeezes mustard out of the tube.

BIEDERMANN What do you mean, judgment of God?

SCHMITZ How should I know?
He eats and glances at the newspaper again.
'— It seems to the experts that the fire was planned
and started in the same manner as last time.'
He laughs briefly, then fills his glass with wine.

ANNA Herr Biedermann?

BIEDERMANN What is it?

ANNA Herr Knechtling would like to speak to you.

BIEDERMANN Knechtling? Now? Knechtling?

ANNA He says —

BIEDERMANN I shouldn't dream of it.

ANNA He says he can't understand you —

BIEDERMANN Why does he have to understand me?

ANNA He has a sick wife and three children —

BIEDERMANN I shouldn't dream of it, I say!
He has jumped to his feet with impatience:
Herr Knechtling! Herr Knechtling! Damn it all,
let Herr Knechtling leave me in peace or instruct
a solicitor I'm taking an evening off. It's ridiculous. I won't put up with all this fuss, just because I gave him the sack! And never before in
human history have we had such social insurance
as we have today ... Yes, let him instruct a solicitor. I'll instruct a solicitor too. A share in his in-

vention! Let him put his head in the gas oven or instruct a solicitor – go ahead – if Herr Knechtling can afford to lose or win a case. Let him try!

He controls himself with a glance at Schmitz.

Tell Herr Knechtling I have a visitor.

Anna goes out.

My apologies!

SCHMITZ This is your house, Herr Biedermann.

BIEDERMANN Is the food all right?

He sits down and watches his guest enjoying himself.

SCHMITZ Who would have thought such a thing still existed nowadays?

BIEDERMANN Mustard?

SCHMITZ Humanity.

He screws the top back on the tube.

I mean who would have believed that you wouldn't grab me by the collar and chuck me out into the street – out into the rain! You see that's what we need, Herr Biedermann: humanity.

He takes the bottle and fills his glass.

God bless you for it.

He drinks with visible enjoyment.

BIEDERMANN You mustn't start thinking now that I'm inhuman, Herr Schmitz –

SCHMITZ Herr Biedermann!

BIEDERMANN That what's Frau Knechtling says!

SCHMITZ If you were inhuman, Herr Biedermann, you wouldn't be giving me shelter tonight, that's obvious.

BIEDERMANN Yes, isn't it?

SCHMITZ Even if it's only in the attic.

He puts down his glass.

Now our wine is just right.

The front door bell rings.

The police – ?

BIEDERMANN My wife –

SCHMITZ H'm.

The bell rings again.

BIEDERMANN Come this way . . . But on one condition: No noise! My wife has a weak heart –

Women's voices are audible from outside and Biedermann beckons to Schmitz to hurry and help him. Taking the tray, glass and bottle with them they tiptoe out right, where the Chorus is sitting.

BIEDERMANN Excuse me.

He steps over the bench.

SCHMITZ Excuse me.

He steps over the bench and they disappear, while Frau Biedermann enters the room from the left accompanied by Anna, who takes her things.

BABETTE Where's my husband? We're not narrow-minded you know, Anna. I don't mind your having a sweetheart, but I won't have you hiding him in the house.

ANNA I haven't got a sweetheart, Frau Biedermann.

BABETTE Then whose is that rusty bicycle by the front door? I got the fright of my life –

ATTIC

Biedermann switches on the light, revealing the attic, and signs to Schmitz to come in. They converse in whispers.

BIEDERMANN Here's the switch . . . If you're cold there's an old sheep-skin rug somewhere, I think – but quiet, for God's sake. . . . Take off your shoes!

Schmitz puts down the tray and takes off one shoe.

Herr Schmitz –

SCHMITZ Herr Biedermann?

BIEDERMANN Will you promise me that you're really not a firebug?

Schmitz can't help laughing.

Sh!

He nods good night, goes out and shuts the door. Schmitz takes off the other shoe.

ROOM

Babette has heard something and listens; she looks horrified, then suddenly relieved; she turns to the audience.

BABETTE My husband Gottlieb has promised me he will personally go up into the attic every evening to make sure there is no firebug there. I'm very grateful to him. If he didn't go I should lie awake half the night . . .

ATTIC

Schmitz goes to the switch, now in his socks, and puts out the light.

. . . .

CHORUS Good people of our city, see
Us, guardians of innocence,
Still free from suspicion,
Filled with good will
Towards the sleeping city,
Sitting,
Standing –
CHORUS LEADER From time to time filling
A pipe to pass the time.
CHORUS Looking,

Listening,
That no fire shall blaze up
From homely roofs
To wipe out our well-beloved city.
A tower-clock strikes three.

CHORUS LEADER Everyone knows we are there and knows
That a call will suffice.
He fills his pipe.

CHORUS Who puts on the light
At this hour of the night?
O woe, I see
With nerves all on edge,
Distressed and sleepless,
The wife.
Babette appears in a dressing-gown.

BABETTE There's someone coughing! . . .
The sound of snoring.
Gottlieb! Can't you hear it?
The sound of coughing.
There's somebody there! . . .
The sound of snoring.
Men! As soon as there's trouble they take a sleeping tablet.
A tower-clock strikes four.

CHORUS LEADER Four o'clock.
Babette puts out the light again.
But no call has come.
He puts his pipe back in his pocket; the background lights up.

CHORUS Beams of the sun,
Lashes of the eye divine,
Day is once more breaking
Above the homely roofs of the city.
    Hail to us!
No ill has befallen the slumbering city,
No ill so far today . . .
    Hail to us!
The Chorus sits down.

2

ROOM

Biedermann is standing with his hat and coat on, a leather briefcase under his arm, drinking his morning coffee and speaking to someone outside the room.

BIEDERMANN For the last time — he isn't a firebug!

VOICE How do you know?

BIEDERMANN I asked him myself . . . And anyhow, can't people think of anything else these days? It's enough to drive one crazy, you and your firebugs the whole time —

Babette comes in with a milk jug.

Enough to drive one crazy!

BABETTE Don't shout at me.

BIEDERMANN I'm not shouting at you, Babette, I'm shouting at people in general.

She pours milk into his cup.

I must go!

He drinks his coffee, which is too hot.

If we take everyone for a firebug, where will it lead to?

We must have a little trust, Babette, a little trust —

He looks at his wrist watch.

BABETTE You're too good-natured. I'm not standing for it, Gottlieb. You let your heart speak, while I can't sleep all night long . . . I shall give him breakfast, but then I shall send him packing, Gottlieb.

BIEDERMANN Do that.

BABETTE In a perfectly friendly way, you know, without hurting his feelings.

BIEDERMANN Do that.

He puts his cup down.

I must go and see my solicitor.

He gives Babette a routine kiss. At this moment

Schmitz appears carrying a sheepskin rug; they don't see him at first.

BABETTE Why did you sack Knechtling?

BIEDERMANN Because I don't need him any more.

BABETTE You were always so satisfied with him.

BIEDERMANN That's what he's trying to make capital out of. A share in his invention! Knechtling knows perfectly well that our hair tonic is the result of salesmanship, not an invention at all. It's ridiculous! The good people who rub our hair tonic on their bald patches might just as well use their own urine –

BABETTE Gottlieb!

BIEDERMANN But it's true!

He makes sure he has everything in his briefcase.

I'm too kind-hearted, you're quite right. I shall twist this Knechtling's neck for him.

He is about to leave, when he sees Schmitz.

SCHMITZ Good morning, sir and madam!

BIEDERMANN Herr Schmitz –

Schmitz stretches out his hand to him.

SCHMITZ Call me Joe!

Biedermann does not take his hand.

BIEDERMANN – my wife will talk to you, Herr Schmitz. I have to go.

Unfortunately. But I wish you all the best . . .

He shakes Schmitz's hand.

All the best, Joe, all the best!

Biedermann leaves.

SCHMITZ All the best, Gottlieb, all the best!

Babette stares at him.

Your husband's name is Gottlieb, isn't it?

BABETTE How did you sleep?

SCHMITZ Cold, thank you. But I took the liberty of wrapping up in the sheepskin rug. – It reminded me of my youth in the charcoal burner's hut . . . Yes – I'm used to the cold . . .

BABETTE Your breakfast is ready.

SCHMITZ Madam!
> *She motions him to the chair.*
This is too much!
> *She fills his cup.*
BABETTE You must have a good meal, Joe. I'm sure you
have a long journey in front of you.
SCHMITZ What do you mean?
> *She motions him to the chair again.*
BABETTE Would you like a soft-boiled egg?
SCHMITZ Two.
BABETTE Anna!
SCHMITZ You see, madam, I feel quite at home already . . .
I make so bold –
> *He sits down. Anna has come in.*
BABETTE Two soft-boiled eggs.
ANNA Very good.
SCHMITZ Three and a half minutes.
ANNA Very good.
> *Anna starts to go.*
SCHMITZ Fräulein!
> *Anna stands in the doorway.*
Good morning!
ANNA Morning.
> *Anna goes out.*
SCHMITZ The way the young lady looks at me! My God, I
believe if it were up to her I should be outside in
the pouring rain!
> *Babette pours coffee.*
BABETTE Herr Schmitz –
SCHMITZ Yes?
BABETTE If I may speak frankly –
SCHMITZ You're trembling, madam!
BABETTE Herr Schmitz –
SCHMITZ What's worrying you?
BABETTE Here's some cheese.
SCHMITZ Thanks.
BABETTE Here's some jam.
SCHMITZ Thanks.

BABETTE Here's some honey.

SCHMITZ One at a time, madam, one at a time!
He leans back and eats his bread and butter, ready to listen.

BABETTE Not to mince matters, Herr Schmitz –

SCHMITZ Call me Joe.

BABETTE Not to mince matters –

SCHMITZ You want to get rid of me?

BABETTE No, Herr Schmitz, no! I wouldn't put it like that –

SCHMITZ Then how would you put it?
He helps himself to cheese.
There's nothing I like better than Tilsiter cheese.
He leans back again and eats, ready to listen.
So madam takes me for a firebug –

BABETTE Don't misunderstand me! What have I said? Nothing is further from my wishes, Herr Schmitz, than to hurt your feelings. Word of honour! You have got me all muddled up. Who said anything about firebugs? I have no complaint whatever to make about your behaviour –
Schmitz puts down his knife and fork.

SCHMITZ I know, I have no manners.

BABETTE No, Herr Schmitz, it's not that –

SCHMITZ A man who makes a noise when he eats –

BABETTE Nonsense –

SCHMITZ They were always telling me that in the orphanage: Schmitz, they used to say, don't make such a din with your dinner!
She picks up the pot to pour coffee.

BABETTE Good heavens, you misunderstand me completely.
He holds his hand over his cup.

SCHMITZ I'm going.

BABETTE Herr Schmitz –

SCHMITZ I'm going.

BABETTE Another cup?
He shakes his head.
Half a cup?

He shakes his head.

You mustn't go like that, Herr Schmitz. I didn't mean to offend you. I didn't say a word about your making a noise when you eat!

He stands up.

Have I offended you?

He folds his table napkin.

SCHMITZ It's not madam's fault if I have no manners. My father was a charcoal burner. Where was I to learn manners? I don't mind hunger and cold, madam – but no education, no manners, madam, no culture . . .

BABETTE I understand.

SCHMITZ I'm going.

BABETTE Where to?

SCHMITZ Out into the rain . . .

BABETTE Oh dear.

SCHMITZ I'm used to it.

BABETTE Herr Schmitz . . . Don't look at me like that! – Your father was a charcoal burner, I see what you mean, Herr Schmitz, I'm sure you had a hard youth –

SCHMITZ No youth at all, madam.

He lowers his eyes and fingers his fingers.

No youth at all. I was seven years old when my mother died . . .

He turns away and wipes his eyes.

BABETTE Joe! – Please Joe . . .

Anna comes in bringing the soft-boiled eggs.

ANNA Anything else?

Anna receives no answer and goes out.

BABETTE I'm not sending you away, Herr Schmitz. I didn't say that at all. What did I say? You really misunderstand me, it's terrible. What can I do to make you believe me?

She hesitantly plucks at his sleeve.

Come on, Joe, eat!

Schmitz sits down at the table again.

What do you take us for? I haven't noticed that
you make a noise when you eat, word of honour!
And even if you did – we set no store by appear-
ances, Herr Schmitz, you must feel that, we're
not that type . . .
He takes the top off his egg.

SCHMITZ God bless you for it!

BABETTE Here's the salt.
He begins to eat the egg.

SCHMITZ It's quite true, madam didn't tell me to leave, not
a word about it, that's quite true. I apologize for
misunderstanding madam . . .

BABETTE Is the egg all right?

SCHMITZ A bit soft . . . I do apologize.
He eats the last spoonful.
What were you going to say, madam, earlier, when
you said: Not to mince matters!

BABETTE Yes, what was I going to say? . . .
He takes the top off the second egg.

SCHMITZ God bless you for it.
He eats the second egg.
Willie always says that private compassion doesn't
exist any more. There aren't any fine people left
nowadays. The State has taken over everything.
There aren't any human beings left. That's what
he says. And that's why the world is going to the
dogs! . . .
He puts salt in the egg.
He'll open his eyes wide when he gets a breakfast
like this, Willie will!
The front door bell rings.
Maybe that's him.
The front door bell rings again.

BABETTE Who is Willie?

SCHMITZ He has culture, madam, you'll see, he used to be
a waiter at the Metropol before it was burnt
down . . .

BABETTE Burnt down?

SCHMITZ   Head waiter.
          Anna has entered.
BABETTE   Who is it?
   ANNA   A gentleman.
BABETTE   What does he want?
   ANNA   From the Fire Insurance, he says; he has to look
          at the house.
          Babette stands up.
          He's wearing tails.
          *Babette and Anna go out, Schmitz pours himself
          coffee.*
SCHMITZ   That must be Willie!

. . . .

         CHORUS   But now there are two
                  That arouse our suspicion,
                  Bicycles, that is to say,
                  Rusty ones, belong to someone,
                  But who?
CHORUS LEADER   One since yesterday, the other since today.
        CHORUS   Woe!
CHORUS LEADER   Once more it is night and we watch.
                A tower-clock strikes.
        CHORUS   The faint-hearted sees much where there's
                nothing,
                Affright at the sight of his shadow,
                Falling over himself
                In excess of zeal.
                Thus in terror he lives
                Till it enters
                Into his very own room.

The tower-clock strikes.

CHORUS LEADER What am I to make of the fact
That these two remain in the house?
The tower-clock strikes.

CHORUS Blinder than blind is the faint-hearted,
Trembling with hope that the thing is not evil
He gives it a friendly reception,
Disarmed, tired out with terror,
Hoping for the best . . .
Until it's too late.
The tower-clock strikes.

CHORUS Woe!
The Chorus sits down.

3

ATTIC

*Schmitz, still in the clothes of a wrestler, and the
Other, who has taken off his tail coat and is wearing
only his white waistcoat, are busy rolling drums into
the attic, tin drums of the sort used to transport
petrol; they have both taken off their shoes and are
being as quiet as possible.*

THE OTHER Quietly! Quietly!

SCHMITZ Suppose it occurs to him to call the police?

THE OTHER Forward!

SCHMITZ What then?

THE OTHER Slowly! Slowly . . . Stop.
*They have rolled the last drum up to others already
standing in the half-light of early morning; the Other
takes cotton-waste and wipes his fingers.*

THE OTHER Why should he call the police?

SCHMITZ Why shouldn't he?

THE OTHER Because he has committed an offence himself.
The cooing of pigeons is heard.

I'm afraid it's day, let's turn in.
He throws away the cotton waste.
Strictly speaking, every citizen above a certain
level of income is guilty of some offence. Don't
worry! . . .
There is a knock on the bolted door.

BIEDERMANN Open up! Open up!
The door is banged and shaken.

THE OTHER That doesn't sound like breakfast.

BIEDERMANN Open the door, I say. Immediately!

SCHMITZ He's never been like that before.
*The banging gets louder and louder. The Other
puts on his tail coat. Without haste, but swiftly, he
straightens his tie and flicks of the dust, then he
opens the door. Biedermann enters in a dressing-
gown, not noticing the newcomer, who has taken up a
position behind the door.*

BIEDERMANN Herr Schmitz!

SCHMITZ Good morning, Herr Biedermann, good morning,
I hope that silly rumbling didn't wake you –

BIEDERMANN Herr Schmitz!

SCHMITZ It shan't happen again.

BIEDERMANN Leave my house.
Pause.
I said, leave my house!

SCHMITZ When?

BIEDERMANN At once.

SCHMITZ Why?

BIEDERMANN Or my wife will ring the police, and I can't and
won't stop her.

SCHMITZ H'm.

BIEDERMANN And at once!
Pause.
What are you waiting for?
Without speaking, Schmitz picks up his shoes.
I don't want any argument!

SCHMITZ I'm not saying anything.

BIEDERMANN If you think I'm going to put up with any old

thing, Herr Schmitz, just because you're a wrest-
ler – that rumbling all night long –
He points with outstretched arm to the door.
Out! Out! I say. Out!
Schmitz addresses the Other.

SCHMITZ He's never been like this before . . .
Biedermann turns round and is speechless.

THE OTHER My name is Eisenring.

BIEDERMANN Gentlemen –?

EISENRING Wilhelm Maria Eisenring.

BIEDERMANN How come there are suddenly two of you, gentle-
men?
Schmitz and Eisenring look at one another.
Without asking!

EISENRING You see?

BIEDERMANN What does that mean?

EISENRING I told you so. You can't do things like that, Joe,
you've got no manners. Without asking. What a
way to behave – suddenly there are two of us.

BIEDERMANN I'm beside myself.

EISENRING You see!
He turns to Biedermann.
I told him so!
He turns to Schmitz.
Didn't I tell you so?
Schmitz looks ashamed of himself.

BIEDERMANN What are you thinking of, gentlemen? I mean to
say, gentlemen, I am the householder. I ask you:
What are you thinking of?
Pause.

EISENRING Answer when the gentleman asks you a question!
Pause.

SCHMITZ Willie is a friend of mine.

BIEDERMANN So what?

SCHMITZ We went to school together, Herr Biedermann,
even as children . . .

BIEDERMANN Well?

SCHMITZ So I thought . . .

BIEDERMANN What?

SCHMITZ So I thought . . .
Pause.

EISENRING You didn't think at all!
He turns to Biedermann.
I understand your feelings perfectly well, Herr
Biedermann, I mean, there's a limit to every-
thing –
He shouts at Schmitz.
Do you imagine a householder has to put up with
absolutely anything?
He turns to Biedermann.
Didn't Joe ask you at all?

BIEDERMANN Not a word!

EISENRING Joe –

BIEDERMANN Not a word!

EISENRING – and then you're surprised when people throw
you out into the street?
*He shakes his head and laughs as though over an
imbecile.*

BIEDERMANN It's not a laughing matter, gentlemen, I'm in
deadly earnest. My wife has a weak heart –

EISENRING You see!

BIEDERMANN My wife was awake half the night. Because of the
rumbling. And anyway, what are you up to here?
He looks around:
What the devil are these drums doing here?
*Schmitz and Eiensring look towards a part of the
attic where there are no drums.*
Over here! Look! What's this?
He bangs a drum.
What's this?

SCHMITZ Drums.

BIEDERMANN Where did they come from?

SCHMITZ Do you know where they came from, Willie?

EISENRING They're imported, it says so on them.

BIEDERMANN Gentlemen –

EISENRING It says so on them somewhere!

Eisenring and Schmitz look for the label.

BIEDERMANN I'm speechless. What an idea! My whole attic full of drums – piled up, positively piled up!

EISENRING That's just it.

BIEDERMANN What do you mean by that?

EISENRING Joe miscalculated . . . Thirty-five by forty-five feet, you said. But the whole attic isn't more than a thousand square feet . . . I can't leave my drums out in the street, Herr Biedermann, you will understand that.

BIEDERMANN I don't understand anything –

Schmitz points to a label.

I'm speechless –

SCHMITZ It tells you here where they come from. Look, here.

BIEDERMANN – simply speechless.

He looks at the label.

DOWN BELOW

Anna conducts a policeman into the room.

ANNA I'll call him.

She goes. The policeman waits.

UP ABOVE

BIEDERMANN Petrol! –

DOWN BELOW

Anna comes back.

ANNA What is it about, sergeant?

POLICEMAN An official matter.

Anna goes. The policeman waits.

UP ABOVE

BIEDERMANN Is that true, gentlemen, is that true?

EISENRING That's what it says on the label. *He shows them the label.*

BEIDERMANN What do you take me for? I've never seen such a thing in my life. Do you imagine I can't read?
They look at the label.
I ask you!–
He speaks like an examining magistrate:
What's in these drums?

EISENRING Petrol.

BIEDERMANN Stop joking! I'm asking you for the last time, what's in these drums? You know as well as I do that an attic isn't the place for petrol –
He runs his finger over the drum:
There – just smell for yourselves!
He holds his finger under their noses:
Is that petrol or isn't it?
They sniff and look at each other.
Answer!

EISENRING It is.

SCHMITZ It is.

BOTH No doubt about it.

BIEDERMANN Are you crazy? My whole attic is full of petrol –

SCHMITZ That's why we aren't smoking, Herr Biedermann.

BIEDERMANN And at a time like this, when there's a warning in every newspaper you open. What are you thinking of? My wife will get a heart attack if she sees this.

EISENRING You see!

BIEDERMANN Don't keep saying, You see, all the time.

EISENRING You can't expect a woman to put up with that, Joe, a housewife. I know housewives –
Anna calls up the stairs.

ANNA Herr Biedermann! Herr Biedermann!
Biedermann shuts the door.

BIEDERMANN Herr Schmitz! Herr –

EISENRING   Eisenring.

BIEDERMANN   If you don't clear these drums out of the house this moment, but this moment, I say –

EISENRING   Then you'll call the police.

BIEDERMANN   Yes.

SCHMITZ   You see!

Anna calls up the stairs.

ANNA   Herr Biedermann!

Biedermann whispers.

BIEDERMANN   That was my last word.

EISENRING   Which one?

BIEDERMANN   I won't stand for petrol in my attic. Once and for all, I won't stand for it!

There is a knock at the door.

I'm coming!

He opens the door to go; a policeman enters.

POLICEMAN   There you are, Herr Biedermann, there you are. You needn't come down, I shan't keep you long.

BIEDERMANN   Good morning!

POLICEMAN   Good morning!

EISENRING   Morning . . .

SCHMITZ   Morning . . .

Schmitz and Eisenring bow.

POLICEMAN   It's about an accident –

BIEDERMANN   Good heavens!

POLICEMAN   An old man whose wife claims that he worked for you – as an inventor! – put his head in the gas oven last night.

He looks in his notebook.

Johann Knechtling, of 11 Horse Lane.

He puts the notebook away.

Did you know anyone of that name?

BIEDERMANN   I –

POLICEMAN   Perhaps you would rather discuss this in private, Herr Biedermann –

BIEDERMANN   Yes.

POLICEMAN   It's no concern of your staff.

BIEDERMANN   No –

He comes to a stop in the doorway.
If anybody asks for me, gentlemen, I shall be at
the police station. All right? I shall be back in a
few minutes.
Schmitz and Eisenring nod.

POLICEMAN Herr Biedermann –

BIEDERMANN Let's go.

POLICEMAN What have you got in those drums?

BIEDERMANN – I?

POLICEMAN If I may ask.

BIEDERMANN ... Hair tonic ...
He looks at Schmitz and Eisenring.

EISENRING HORMOFLOR.

SCHMITZ 'Fresh hope for men.'

EISENRING HORMOFLOR.

SCHMITZ 'Try it today.'

EISENRING 'Restore your hair the Hormoflor way.'

BOTH HORMOFLOR, HORMOFLOR, HORMOFLOR.
The policeman laughs.

BIEDERMANN Is he dead?
Biedermann and the policeman go.

EISENRING A charming fellow.

SCHMITZ Didn't I tell you so?

EISENRING But not a word about breakfast. . . .

SCHMITZ He's never been like that before.
Eisenring puts a hand in his trouser pocket.

EISENRING Have you got the primer?
Schmitz puts a hand in his trouser pocket.

SCHMITZ He's never been like that before . . .

. . . .

CHORUS Beams of the sun,
Lashes of the eye divine,

Day is once more breaking
Above the homely roofs of the city.
CHORUS LEADER Today as yesterday.
CHORUS Hail to us!
CHORUS LEADER No ill has befallen the slumbering city.
CHORUS Hail to us!
CHORUS LEADER No ill so far . . .
CHORUS Hail to us!
The sound of traffic, hooters, trams.
CHORUS LEADER Clever is man and master of many dangers.
When he thinks
Upon that which he sees.
When his mind is alert he observes
The signs of approaching disaster
In time if he will.
CHORUS But suppose he will not?
CHORUS LEADER He who, in order to know
What danger threatens, reads papers,
Each day at breakfast indignant
Over some distant disaster,
Each day given explanations
That spare him the need to think,
Each day informed of what happened the day
before,
He finds it hard to perceive what is happening
now
Beneath his own roof –
CHORUS Unpublished!
CHORUS LEADER Manifest.
CHORUS Scandalous!
CHORUS LEADER True.
CHORUS Unwilling he is to see through it, for then –
*The Chorus Leader interrupts the Chorus with a
gesture of the hand.*
CHORUS LEADER Here he comes.
The Chorus wheels round.
CHORUS No ill has befallen the slumbering city,
Today as yesterday,

As a means of forgetting
The danger that threatens
The citizen rushes,
Cleanly shaved,
To his office . . .
Biedermann appears in overcoat and hat, his brief-case under his arm.

BIEDERMANN Taxi! . . . Taxi? . . . Taxi!
The Chorus blocks his path.
What's the matter?

CHORUS Woe!

BIEDERMANN What do you want?

CHORUS Woe!

BIEDERMANN You've said that already.

CHORUS Thrice woe!

BIEDERMANN What do you mean?

CHORUS LEADER Deeply suspicious, we think
The danger of fire is revealed
To our eyes as to yours.
How am I to construe
Drums full of fuel in the attic.
Biedermann yells.

BIEDERMANN Mind your own business!
Silence.
Let me pass. – I have to see my solicitor. – What
do you want with me? – I've done no wrong . . .
Biedermann appears to be frightened.
Is this a cross-examination?
Biedermann displays masterful self-assurance.
Stand aside.
The Chorus stands motionless.

CHORUS Never beseems it the Chorus
To sit in judgment upon
Citizens who take action.

CHORUS LEADER The Chorus sees from without
And thus more quickly perceives
The peril that threatens.

CHORUS Questioning merely, polite

Even when danger dismays us,
Warning merely, restrained
In spite of our anguish,
Helpless though watchful, the Chorus
Offers its help till the fire
Is beyond all hope of extinction.
Biedermann looks at his wrist-watch.

BIEDERMANN I'm in a hurry.

CHORUS Woe!

BIEDERMANN I really don't know what you want.

CHORUS LEADER Biedermann Gottlieb, explain
Why all those drums full of fuel
In your loft you allow to remain.

BIEDERMANN Explain?

CHORUS LEADER Knowing full well how inflammable
The world is, what did you think?

BIEDERMANN Think?
He eyes the Chorus:
Gentlemen, I am a free citizen. I can think what I like. What is the meaning of all these questions? I have a right not to think anything at all, gentlemen – quite apart from the fact that what happens under my roof is my business, I mean to say, I am the house-owner! . . .

CHORUS Sacred to us what is sacred,
Property,
Even if out of it springs
A fire that we cannot extinguish
That reduces us all to a cinder,
Sacred to us what is sacred!

BIEDERMANN Very well, then. –
Silence.
Why don't you let me pass?
Silence.
People shouldn't always think the worst. Where will that lead? I want peace and quiet, that's all, and as to the two gentlemen – quite apart from the fact that I have other worries just now . . .

Enter Babette in hat and coat.

What are you doing here?

BABETTE Am I in the way?

BIEDERMANN I'm in conference with the Chorus.

Babette nods to the Chorus, then whispers in Biedermann's ear.

BIEDERMANN Of course with a ribbon! It doesn't matter what it costs so long as it's a wreath.

Babette nods to the Chorus.

BABETTE Excuse me, gentlemen.

Babette leaves.

BIEDERMANN In short, gentlemen, I've had enough of you and your firebugs! I never go to the local any more, I'm fed up with it. Can't people find anything else to talk about nowadays? After all, I've only got one life. If we take everyone we meet, except ourselves, for a firebug, how are things ever going to improve? Damn it all, we must have a little trust, a little good will. That's what I think. We mustn't always look on the black side. Damn it all, not everybody is a firebug. That's what I think. A little trust, a little . . .

Pause.

I can't be scared the whole time!

Pause.

Do you think I slept a wink last night? I'm no fool. Petrol is petrol! The grimmest thoughts filled my mind – I climbed up onto the table to listen, and later even onto the cupboard to put my ear to the ceiling. They were snoring. Snoring! At least four times I climbed up onto the cupboard. Peacefully snoring! . . . But in spite of that, believe it or not, I once went out onto the landing, in my pyjamas – I was so furious. I was on the point of throwing the two scoundrels out into the street – along with their drums – with my own hands, ruthlessly, in the middle of the night!

CHORUS With your own hands?

BIEDERMANN Yes.

CHORUS Ruthlessly?

BIEDERMANN Yes.

CHORUS In the middle of the night?

BIEDERMANN I was just on the point of doing so, yes – if my wife hadn't come out because she was afraid I should catch cold – just on the point, I was!
He takes a cigar to hide his embarrassment.

CHORUS LEADER How am I to explain it?
He spent a sleepless night.
Did it cross his mind that they might
Abuse the citizen's kindness?
Seized with suspicion he was. Why was that?
Biedermann lights his cigar.

CHORUS What troubles beset the citizen
Who, though hard as nails in business,
Is elsewhere a charming fellow,
Anxious
To do good.

CHORUS LEADER When it suits him.

CHORUS Hoping that good will come
From good-natured actions,
A sadly mistaken assumption.

BIEDERMANN What do you mean?

CHORUS To us the place reeks of petrol.
Biedermann sniffs.

BIEDERMANN Well, gentlemen, I can't smell anything . . .

CHORUS Alas!

BIEDERMANN Nothing whatever.

CHORUS Alas!

CHORUS LEADER So used already is he
To evil stenches.

CHORUS Alas!

BIEDERMANN Don't be so defeatist all the time, gentlemen: stop saying Alas! all the time.
A car hoots.
Taxi! – Taxi!
A car can be heard stopping.

Excuse me.
Biedermann hurries off.

CHORUS Citizen—where are you going?
A car is heard starting up.

CHORUS LEADER What is he planning to do,
The unhappy man?
Afraid and reckless,
I thought, and pale in the face,
He hurried away,
Afraid and determined – what is he planning to
do?
A car is heard hooting.

CHORUS So used already is he
To evil stenches!
The car is heard hooting in the distance.
Alas!

CHORUS LEADER Alack!
*The Chorus withdraws, with the exception of the
Leader, who takes out his pipe.*

CHORUS LEADER He who fears change
More than disaster,
What can he do to forestall
The threatening disaster?
He follows the Chorus.

4

ATTIC

*Eisenring, alone, is unwinding cord from a reel,
whistling "Lili Marlene" as he works. He stops
whistling to wet his index finger and hold it
up out of the skylight to test the direction of the
wind.*

ROOM

Enter Biedermann, followed by Babette. He takes off his coat and throws down the briefcase, a cigar in his mouth.

BIEDERMANN Do as I tell you.

BABETTE A goose?

BIEDERMANN A goose.
He takes off his tie, the cigar in his mouth.

BABETTE Why are you taking off your tie, Gottlieb?
He hands her the tie.

BIEDERMANN If I report those two to the police, then I know I shall make enemies of them. What's the good of that? One match, and our whole house will be in flames. What's the good of that? But if I go up and invite them to supper – and they accept my invitation . . .

BABETTE What then?

BIEDERMANN Then we shall be friends. –
He takes off his jacket, hands it to his wife and goes out.

BABETTE Anna, you won't be able to take this evening off. We're having visitors. Lay the table for four.

ATTIC

Eisenring is singing "Lili Marlene," then there is a knock at the door.

EISENRING Come in.
He goes on whistling, but no one comes in.
Come in.
Enter Biedermann in shirtsleeves, his cigar in his hand.
Morning, Herr Biedermann.

BIEDERMANN May I?

EISENRING How did you sleep?

BIEDERMANN Wretchedly, thank you.

EISENRING Me too. It's that south wind . . .
He continues working with the cord and the reel.
BIEDERMANN I hope I'm not disturbing you.
EISENRING But of course not, Herr Biedermann, you're at home here.
BIEDERMANN I don't want to be in the way.
The cooing of pigeons is heard.
Where has our friend got to?
EISENRING Joe? At work, the lazy dog. He didn't want to go without breakfast! I sent him to get some wood-wool.
BIEDERMANN Wood-wool –?
EISENRING Wood-wool carries the sparks furthest.
Biedermann laughs faintly as though at a poor joke.
BIEDERMANN What I was going to say, Herr Eisenring –
EISENRING Are you going to throw us out again?
BIEDERMANN In the middle of the night (my sleeping tablets are all gone) it suddenly occurred to me that you haven't a toilet up here –
EISENRING We have the gutter.
BIEDERMANN As you like, gentlemen, as you like. It just crossed my mind. All night long. Perhaps you'd like to wash or take a shower. Don't hesitate to use my bathroom. I told Anna to put out towels for you.
Eisenring shakes his head.
Why do you shake your head?
EISENRING Where on earth has he put it?
BIEDERMANN What?
EISENRING Have you seen a primer anywhere?
He looks here and there.
Don't worry about the bathroom, Herr Bieder-mann. Seriously. There was no bathroom in prison either, you know.
BIEDERMANN Prison?
EISENRING Didn't Joe tell you I had just come out of prison?
BIEDERMANN No.
EISENRING Not a word?

BIEDERMANN No.

EISENRING He talks of nothing but himself all the time. There are people like that. I mean, is it our fault that he had such a tragic youth? Did you have a tragic youth, Herr Biedermann? I didn't! – I could have gone to the university, Father wanted me to be a lawyer.

He stands at the skylight conversing with the pigeons: Grrr! Grrr! Grrr!

Biedermann re-lights his cigar.

BIEDERMANN Herr Eisenring, I didn't sleep all night. Tell me frankly, is there really petrol in those drums?

EISENRING Don't you trust us?

BIEDERMANN I'm only asking.

EISENRING What do you take us for, Herr Biedermann, tell me frankly, what do you take us for?

BIEDERMANN You mustn't think I have no sense of humour, my friend, but the kind of jokes you make are really a bit much.

EISENRING That's something we've learnt.

BIEDERMANN What is?

EISENRING Joking is the third best method of hoodwinking people. The second best is sentimentality. The kind of stuff our Joe goes in for – a childhood with charcoal burners in the forest, an orphanage, the circus and so on. But the best and safest method – in my opinion – is to tell the plain un-varnished truth. Oddly enough. No one believes it.

ROOM

Anna brings in Widow Knechtling all in black.

ANNA Sit down.

The Widow sits down.

But if you're Frau Knechtling, you're wasting your time. Herr Biedermann said he wouldn't have anything to do with you –

The Widow stands up.
Sit down.
The Widow sits down.
But I'm afraid you're going to be disappointed. . .
Anna goes out.

ATTIC

Eisenring is standing working, Biedermann is stand-ing smoking.

EISENRING What on earth is keeping Joe so long? Wood-wool is easy enough to get hold of. I hope they haven't nabbed him.

BIEDERMANN Nabbed him?

EISENRING Why does that amuse you?

BIEDERMANN You know, when you talk like that, Herr Eisen-ring, you seem to me to come from another world. Nabbed! I find it fascinating. From another world! I mean, in the circles in which we move people hardly ever get nabbed –

EISENRING Because in such circles people don't steal wood-wool, that's obvious, Herr Biedermann, that's class distinction.

BIEDERMANN Nonsense!

EISENRING You don't mean, Herr Biedermann –

BIEDERMANN I don't believe in class distinctions! – You must have felt that, Eisenring, I'm not old-fashioned. On the contrary. I'm genuinely sorry that among the lower classes people still blather about class distinctions. Aren't we all creatures of one creator nowadays, whether we're rich or poor? The middle class too. Aren't we both flesh and blood, you and I? . . . I don't know, Herr Eisen-ring, whether you also smoke cigars?
He offers one, but Eisenring shakes his head.
I don't say all men are equal, of course; there will always be the competent and the incompetent,

thank God; but why don't we just shake hands?
A little good will, damn it all, a little idealism, a
little – and we could all live in peace, rich and
poor, don't you agree?

EISENRING If I may be frank, Herr Biedermann –

BIEDERMANN Please do.

EISENRING You won't take it amiss?

BIEDERMANN The franker the better.

EISENRING I mean, quite frankly, you ought not to smoke
here.

Biedermann starts and puts out his cigar.

It's not for me to tell you what to do here, Herr
Biedermann, after all this is your house, but you
understand –

BIEDERMANN Of course!

Eisenring bends down.

EISENRING There it is!

*He picks something up from the floor and blows it
clean before attaching it to the cord, once more
whistling "Lili Marlene."*

BIEDERMANN Tell me, Herr Eisenring: What are you doing all
the time? If I may ask. And what's that thing?

EISENRING The primer.

BIEDERMANN –?

EISENRING And that's the fuse.

BIEDERMANN –?

EISENRING There are supposed to be even better ones now,
Joe says, new models. But they're not in the
arsenals yet, and it's out of the question for us
to buy them. Everything connected with war is
terribly expensive, nothing but the top quality.

BIEDERMANN Fuse, you say?

EISENRING Detonating fuse.

He gives Biedermann one end of the fuse:

Will you be so kind as to hold this end, Herr
Biedermann, so that I can measure it?

Biedermann holds the fuse.

BIEDERMANN Joking apart, my friend –

EISENRING Only for a moment!
He whistles "Lili Marlene" and measures the fuse.
Thanks, Herr Biedermann, thanks very much.
Biedermann bursts out laughing.

BIEDERMANN No, Willie, you can't kid me. Not me! But I must say you put a great deal of trust in people's sense of humour. A great deal! If you talk like that I can well believe you get arrested now and then. Not everyone has as much sense of humour as I have, my friend!

EISENRING We have to find the right people.

BIEDERMANN At the local, for instance, they fly off the handle if you so much as say you believe in the goodness in man.

EISENRING Ha.

BIEDERMANN And yet I donated a sum to our Fire Brigade so big I won't even tell you how much it was.

EISENRING Ha.
He lays the fuse.
The people who have no sense of humour are just as lost when the balloon goes up; don't worry about that!
Biedermann has to sit down on a drum, sweating.
What's the matter, Herr Biedermann? You're quite pale!
He slaps him on the back.
I know, it's this smell, when you're not used to the smell of petrol it can upset you – I'll open a window.
Eisenring opens the door.

BIEDERMANN Thank you . . .
Anna calls up the stairs.

ANNA Herr Biedermann! Herr Biedermann!

EISENRING The police again?

ANNA Herr Biedermann!

EISENRING If this isn't a police state, what is it?

ANNA Herr Biedermann –

BIEDERMANN Coming!

In a whisper:
Herr Eisenring, do you like goose?

EISENRING Goose?

BIEDERMANN Goose, yes, goose.

EISENRING Like? Me? Why?

BIEDERMANN With chestnut stuffing?

EISENRING And red cabbage?

BIEDERMANN Yes ... What I meant to say was, my wife and I –
especially I – thought if you would like ... I
don't want to be a nuisance! – if you would like to
come to dinner, Herr Eisenring, you and Joe –

EISENRING Tonight?

BIEDERMANN Or would you rather come tomorrow?

EISENRING I don't think we shall be here tomorrow. But
tonight with pleasure, Herr Biedermann, with
pleasure!

BIEDERMANN Shall we say seven o'clock?
Anna calls up the stairs.

ANNA Herr Biedermann!
He shakes hands with Eisenring.

BIEDERMANN Is that a date?

EISENRING It's a date.
*Biedermann goes and stops once more in the door-
way, giving a friendly nod while he glances glumly
at the drums and fuse. It's a date!*
*Biedermann goes and Eisenring carries on with his
work, whistling. The Chorus steps forward as though
the scene were at an end; but just as the Chorus has
gathered by the footlights there is a crash in the
attic; something has fallen over.*

ATTIC

EISENRING You can come out, doctor.
*A Third crawls out from between the drums, a man
wearing glasses.*
You heard, didn't you? Joe and I have got to go

out to supper. You'll be on watch here. See no one comes in and smokes. Got it? Before the proper time.

The Third polishes his glasses, silent and serious. Eisenring laughs.

I often wonder, doctor, what you're really doing along with us, when you don't get any kick out of a fine blaze, sparks and crackling flames, out of sirens that are always too late, barking dogs and human cries – and ashes.

The Third puts on his glasses, silent and serious. Eisenring laughs.

World reformer!

He whistles for a while to himself without looking at the Doctor of Philosophy.

I don't like you academic types, but you know that, doctor, I told you so at the outset: there's no real fun in it, you lot are always so ideological, so serious, to the point of treachery – there's no real fun in it.

He continues working and whistling.

. . . .

CHORUS Ready are we,
Carefully coiled are the hoses,
In accordance with regulations,
Polished and carefully greased and of brass
Is each windlass.
Everyone knows what his task is.
CHORUS LEADER An ill wind is blowing –
CHORUS Everyone knows what his task is,

Polished and carefully tested,
To make sure that we have full pressure,
And likewise of brass is our pump.

CHORUS LEADER And the hydrants?

CHORUS Ready are we. –

Babette enters carrying a goose, accompanied by the Ph.D.

BABETTE Yes, doctor, I know, but my husband – yes, doctor, I know it's urgent, yes, I'll tell him –

She leaves the doctor standing and moves forward to the footlights.

My husband has ordered a goose, look, here it is. And I'm supposed to roast it! So that we can get friendly with that lot up there.

The sound of church bells.

It's Saturday evening, as you can hear, and I can't get rid of a silly presentiment that maybe they're ringing for the last time, the bells of our city . . .

Biedermann shouts for Babette.

I don't know, ladies, whether Gottlieb is always right. This is what he once said: Of course they're scoundrels, but if I make enemies of them then it's all up with our hair restorer! And no sooner was he in the Party –

Biedermann shouts for Babette.

It's always the same! I know my Gottlieb. He's always too kind-hearted, just too kind-hearted!

Babette leaves with the goose.

CHORUS One wearing glasses.
A boy of good family doubtless,
Not given to envy,
But full of book-learning and pale,
No longer hopeful that good
Will come of good-nature,
But resolved to perform any action,
Convinced as he is that the end
Justifies fully the means,

Oh,
Hopeful he too . . . Man of good will and of ill.
Cleaning his glasses to lengthen his view
He sees in the drums full of fuel
Not fuel –
He sees the idea!
Till all's blazing.

PH.D. Good evening . . .

CHORUS LEADER Man the hoses!
Man the pumps!
Man the ladders!
The Firemen run to their places.
Good evening.
*To the audience, after calls of 'Be ready!' have
echoed from all sides:*
We are ready. –

5

ROOM

*Widow Knechtling is still there; she is standing.
The ringing of bells is heard very loud. Anna is
laying the table and Biedermann brings two chairs.*

BIEDERMANN – Because, as you can see, I haven't time, Frau
Knechtling, I haven't time to bother with the
dead – as I said: Get in touch with my solicitor.
Widow Knechtling goes.
One can't hear oneself speak, Anna, shut the
window!
Anna shuts the window; the ringing grows fainter.
I told you I wanted everything plain and simple,
a simple supper in a free and easy atmosphere.
What are these idiotic candelabra doing?

ANNA But we always have those, Herr Biedermann.

BIEDERMANN Plain and simple, free and easy, I said. No ostentation! – And these finger bowls, for God's sake, silver, nothing but silver and cut glass everywhere. What kind of an impression is that going to make? *He picks up the knife-rests and puts them in his pocket.*

Can't you see I'm wearing my oldest jacket, Anna – And you . . . Leave the big poultry knife, Anna, we shall need that. But apart from that, away with all this silver! I want the two gentlemen to feel at home . . . Where's the corkscrew?

ANNA Here.

BIEDERMANN Haven't we something simpler?

ANNA In the kitchen, but it's rusty.

BIEDERMANN Bring it here!
He takes a silver bucket from the table.
What the hell's this for?

ANNA For the wine –

BIEDERMANN Silver!
He stares at the bucket and then at Anna:
Do we always have this?

ANNA Yes, you need it, Herr Biedermann.

BIEDERMANN Need! What do you mean, need? What we need is humanity, brotherhood. Away with it! – And what the hell have you got there?

ANNA Table napkins.

BIEDERMANN Damask!

ANNA We haven't any others.
He picks up the table napkins and puts them in the silver bucket.

BIEDERMANN There are whole tribes that live without table napkins, human beings like ourselves –
Enter Babette with a large wreath. Biedermann hasn't noticed her yet; he is standing by the table:
I ask myself what we need a tablecloth for at all –

BABETTE Gottlieb?

BIEDERMANN At all costs no class distinctions!
He sees Babette.
What's that wreath?

BABETTE It's the one we ordered. What do you think of that, Gottlieb, they've sent the wreath here. And yet I wrote out the address for them myself, Knechtling's address, in black and white. And they've got the ribbon and everything the wrong way round!

BIEDERMANN The ribbon? What do you mean?

BABETTE And the boy says they've sent the bill to Frau Knechtling.

She shows him the ribbon:

TO OUR UNFORGETTABLE GOTTLIEB BIEDER-
MANN.

He looks at the ribbon.

BIEDERMANN We're not accepting that. Certainly not! They'll have to change it –

He goes back to the table:

Don't worry me now, Babette, I've got other things to do. Damn it all, I can't be everywhere.

Babette goes with the wreath.

Right, get rid of the tablecloth! Give me a hand, Anna. And as I said, no waiting at table. Under no circumstances. Come in without knocking, just come straight in, and simply put the pan on the table –

ANNA The pan?

He removes the tablecloth.

BIEDERMANN That immediately creates a completely different atmosphere. You see? A bare wooden table, no fripperies, as at the Last Supper.

He gives her the tablecloth.

ANNA You mean I'm to bring the goose in the pan, Herr Biedermann?

She folds up the tablecloth.

What wine shall I bring, Herr Biedermann?

BIEDERMANN I'll fetch that myself.

ANNA Herr Biedermann!

BIEDERMANN What is it?

ANNA I haven't got a sweater like you said, Herr

Biedermann, a simple sweater that makes me look like one of the family.

BIEDERMANN Borrow one from my wife!

ANNA The yellow one or the red one?

BIEDERMANN It doesn't matter. But I don't want any show – no cap and no apron. You understand? And as I said: Get rid of these candelabra! And see that things don't look so dreadfully neat and tidy here! . . . I'm going down to the cellar.

Biedermann goes out.

ANNA 'See that things don't look so dreadfully neat and tidy here' indeed!

After folding it, she hurls the tablecloth into a corner and stamps on it with both feet.

Anything you say!

Enter Schmitz and Eisenring, each carrying a rose.

BOTH Good evening, Fräulein!

Anna goes out without looking at them.

EISENRING Why no wood-wool?

SCHMITZ Confiscated. By the police. As a safety measure. Anyone selling or possessing wood-wool without a police permit will be arrested. A precaution being taken throughout the country . . .

He combs his hair.

EISENRING Have you any matches left?

SCHMITZ Not me.

EISENRING Nor me.

Schmitz blows through his comb.

SCHMITZ We'll have to ask him for some.

EISENRING Biedermann?

SCHMITZ Mustn't forget.

He puts the comb away and sniffs.

M'm, it smells good! . . .

Biedermann comes to the footlights carrying a bottle.

BIEDERMANN You can think what you like about me, gentlemen. But just answer one question:

The sound of raucous singing and laughter.

I tell myself: So long as they're bawling and booz-

ing they're not doing anything else . . . The best
bottles in my cellar – if anyone had told me a week
ago –. Tell me the honest truth, gentlemen; When
exactly did you know for sure that they were
firebugs? It doesn't come the way you think,
gentlemen – it comes first slowly and then
suddenly . . . Suspicion! I was suspicious from
the beginning, one is always suspicious – but tell
me honestly, gentlemen, what would you have
done in my place, damn it all, and when?

He listens. There is silence.

I must go up!

He hurries away.

6

ROOM

*The goose-dinner is in full swing; laughter, Bieder-
mann especially (still carrying the bottle) cannot get
over the joke that has just been made; only Babette
is not laughing at all.*

BIEDERMANN Cotton-waste! Did you hear that? Cotton-waste,
he says, cotton-waste burns better still!

BABETTE What's funny about that?

BIEDERMANN Cotton-waste! – do you know what cotton-waste
is?

BABETTE Yes.

BIEDERMANN You've no sense of humour, Babette.

He puts the bottle on the table.

What can you do, my friends, when a person has
no sense of humour?

BABETTE All right, explain the joke to me.

BIEDERMANN Well, it's like this. Willie told me this morning he
had sent Joe to steal wood-wool. Wood-wool,
got it? Just now I asked Joe: How's the wood-
wool? To which he replied that he hadn't been

able to organize any wood-wool, but he'd picked up some cotton-waste. Got it? And Willie said: Cotton-waste burns far better!

BABETTE I got that.

BIEDERMANN Oh, you got that, did you?

BABETTE And what's funny about it?

Biedermann gives up.

BIEDERMANN Let's drink, gentlemen!

Biedermann uncorks the bottle.

BABETTE Is it true, Herr Schmitz, that you have put cotton-waste up in our attic?

BIEDERMANN You'll laugh, Babette, but this morning we actually measured the fuse together, Willie and I.

BABETTE Fuse?

BIEDERMANN Detonating fuse!

He fills the glasses.

BABETTE But now seriously, gentlemen, what's all this about?

Biedermann laughs.

BIEDERMANN Seriously, she says! Seriously! Did you hear that? Seriously! . . . Don't let them kid you, Babette; I told you, our friends have a way of joking – other circles, other jokes, I always say . . . They'll be asking me for matches next!

Schmitz and Eisenring exchange glances.

You know, the two gentlemen still take me for a nervous suburbanite with no sense of humour who can be scared – *He raises his glass:*

Cheers!

EISENRING Cheers!

SCHMITZ Cheers!

They rise and clink glasses.

BIEDERMANN To our friendship.

They drink and sit down again.

We don't have anyone waiting at table in our house, gentlemen, just tuck in.

SCHMITZ I simply can't eat any more.

EISENRING Go on, Joe, don't be shy. You're not in the orphanage now.
He helps himself to goose.
Your goose is first-class, madam.

BABETTE I'm glad.

EISENRING Goose and Pommard! – The only thing missing is a tablecloth.

BABETTE Did you hear that, Gottlieb?

EISENRING But we can manage without it – A white tablecloth, you know, damask with silver on it.

BIEDERMANN Anna!

EISENRING Damask with flowers in it, but white, you know, like frost flowers! – But we can manage without it, Herr Biedermann. We didn't have a tablecloth in prison either.

BIEDERMANN Anna!

BABETTE In prison –?

BIEDERMANN Where has she got to?

BABETTE Have you been in prison?
Anna comes; she is wearing a bright red sweater.

BIEDERMANN Bring a tablecloth at once!

ANNA Very good –

EISENRING And if you have something like finger bowls –

ANNA Very good –

EISENRING You may think it childish, madam, but that's what the common people are like. Take Joe, for instance, who grew up among the charcoal burners and has never seen a knife-rest – the dream of his ruined life is a table laid with silver and cut glass!

BABETTE Gottlieb, we have all that.

EISENRING But we can manage without it.

ANNA As you wish.

EISENRING And if you have table napkins, Fräulein, bring them here!

ANNA Herr Biedermann said –

BIEDERMANN Bring them here!

ANNA As you wish.
Anna brings everything back.

EISENRING I hope you won't take it amiss, madam. When you
come out of prison, you know, after months with-
out civilization –
He takes the tablecloth and shows it to Schmitz:
Do you know what that is?
Speaking to Babette:
He's never seen such a thing before!
To Schmitz again:
That's damask.

SCHMITZ Well, what am I supposed to do with it?
Eisenring ties the tablecloth round his neck.

EISENRING Like this –
Biedermann tries to see the funny side and laughs.

BABETTE And where are our knife-rests, Anna, where have
our knife-rests got to?

ANNA Herr Biedermann –

BIEDERMANN Bring them here!

ANNA You said: Take them away.

BIEDERMANN Bring them here, I say! Where are they, in
heaven's name?

ANNA In your left trouser pocket.

EISENRING Don't excite yourself.
Biedermann puts his hand in his pocket and finds them.

ANNA It's not my fault.

EISENRING Don't excite yourself, Fraulein –
Anna bursts out sobbing, turns and runs out.
It's this south wind that does it.
Pause.

BIEDERMANN Drink, my friends, drink!
They drink in silence.

EISENRING I used to eat goose every day, you know, when I
was a waiter. When you flit down the long corri-
dors with the dish on the palm of your hand. But
then, madam, where are we to wipe our fingers?
That's the problem. Where else but in our own
hair? – while other people have cut-glass finger
bowls for the purpose! That's what I shall never
forget.

He dips his fingers into the finger bowl.

Do you know what a trauma is?

BIEDERMANN No.

EISENRING They explained it all to me in prison . . .

He dries his fingers.

BABETTE Tell me, Herr Eisenring, what did you go to prison for?

BIEDERMANN Babette!

EISENRING What did I go to prison for?

BIEDERMANN One doesn't ask such questions!

EISENRING I ask myself . . . I was a waiter, as I told you, a little head-waiter, and suddenly they confused me with a big firebug.

BIEDERMANN H'm.

EISENRING Arrested me in my home.

BIEDERMANN H'm.

EISENRING I was so taken aback that I did as they told me.

BIEDERMANN H'm.

EISENRING I was lucky, madam, I had seven absolutely charming policemen. When I said, I had to go to work and had no time to spare, they said: Your restaurant has been burnt down.

BIEDERMANN Burnt down?

EISENRING Overnight, it seems, yes.

BABETTE Burnt down?

EISENRING Fine! I thought. Then I've got time on my hands. The restaurant was nothing but a smouldering skeleton. I saw it as I went past, you know, out of that little barred window in the prison van.

He drinks with the air of a connoisseur.

We used to have that too: Forty-nine! Cave de l'Echannon . . . What happened then? Joe must tell you about that. As I was sitting in the ante-room playing with the handcuffs, who should walk in but this fellow!

Schmitz beams.

Cheers, Joe!

SCHMITZ Cheers, Willie!

They drink.

BIEDERMANN Then what happened?

SCHMITZ Are you the firebug? they asked him and offered him a cigarette. Sorry, he said, I'm afraid I haven't any matches, superintendent, although you take me for a firebug — *They laugh uproariously and slap their thighs.*

BIEDERMANN H'm.

Anna has come in. She is wearing a cap and apron again, and hands Biedermann a visiting-card which he looks at.

ANNA It's urgent, he says.

BIEDERMANN But I have guests —

Schmitz and Eisenring clink glasses again.

SCHMITZ Cheers, Willie!

EISENRING Cheers, Joe!

They drink. Biedermann studies the visiting-card.

BABETTE Who is it, Gottlieb?

BIEDERMANN The Doctor of Philosophy . . .

Anna is busy at the sideboard.

EISENRING What's that other thing there, Fräulein, that silver thing?

ANNA The candelabra?

EISENRING Why are you hiding it?

BIEDERMANN Bring it here!

ANNA Herr Biedermann, you told me yourself —

BIEDERMANN Bring it here, I say!

Anna puts the candelabra on the table.

EISENRING Joe, what do you say to that? They have a candelabra and hide it! What more do you want? Silver with candles on it . . . Have you any matches?

He puts his hand in his trouser pocket.

SCHMITZ Me? No.

He puts his hand in his trouser pocket.

EISENRING I'm afraid we haven't any matches, Herr Biedermann, really we haven't.

BIEDERMANN I have.

EISENRING Give them here!

BIEDERMANN I'll do it. Leave it to me! I'll do it.
He lights the candles.

BABETTE What does the gentleman want?

ANNA I can't make out, madam. He can't keep silent any longer, he says, and he's waiting on the landing.

BABETTE Confidentially, he says?

ANNA Yes, he keeps saying he wants to make a disclosure.

BABETTE What disclosure?

ANNA I can't make that out, madam, however often he tells me. He says he wants to dissociate himself . . .
Many candles blaze.

EISENRING It creates a completely different impression all at once, don't you agree, madam? Candlelight.

BABETTE Oh yes.

EISENRING I like atmosphere.

BIEDERMANN You know, Herr Eisenring, I'm glad to hear that . . .
All the candles are lit.

EISENRING Schmitz, don't make such a din with your dinner!
Babette takes Eisenring on one side.

BABETTE Let him be!

EISENRING He has no manners, madam, I apologize; I find it terribly embarrassing. But where could he have learnt manners? From the charcoal burner's hut to the orphanage –

BABETTE I know!

EISENRING From the orphanage to the circus –

BABETTE I know!

EISENRING From the circus to the theatre.

BABETTE I didn't know that, no –

EISENRING Human destinies, madam, human destinies!
Babette turns to Schmitz.

BABETTE So you were in the theatre too?
Schmitz, gnawing a goose bone, nods.

Where was that?

SCHMITZ Backstage.

EISENRING And yet he's gifted – Joe as a ghost, have you ever
seen that?

SCHMITZ But not now!

EISENRING Why not?

SCHMITZ I was only with the theatre for a week, madam,
then it was burnt down –

BABETTE Burnt down?

EISENRING Come on! Don't be shy!

BIEDERMANN Burnt down?

EISENRING Don't be shy!

*He unties the tablecloth which Schmitz has been
wearing like a table napkin and throws it over
Schmitz's head.*

Go ahead!

Schmitz, covered by the white tablecloth, rises.

See? Doesn't he look like a ghost?

ANNA I'm frightened.

EISENRING Girlie!

*He takes Anna in his arms; she covers her face with
her hands.*

SCHMITZ 'Can we?'

EISENRING That's theatrical language, madam, he learnt it
during the rehearsals in a single week, before the
theatre was burnt down, believe it or not!

BABETTE Don't keep talking about fires all the time!

SCHMITZ 'Can we?'

EISENRING Ready. –

All sit, Eisenring holding Anna to his breast.

SCHMITZ EVERYMAN! EVERYMAN!

BABETTE Gottlieb –?

BIEDERMANN Quiet!

BABETTE We saw that at Salzburg.

SCHMITZ BIEDERMANN! BIEDERMANN!

EISENRING I think it's wonderful the way he does that.

SCHMITZ BIEDERMANN! BIEDERMANN!

EISENRING You must ask: Who are you?

BIEDERMANN Me?

EISENRING Otherwise he won't be able to get through his words.

SCHMITZ EVERYMAN! BIEDERMANN!

BIEDERMANN All right, then: who am I?

BABETTE No, you must ask who he is.

BIEDERMANN Oh, I see.

SCHMITZ DO YOU NOT HEAR ME?

EISENRING No, Joe, take it again from the beginning!
They take up fresh positions.

SCHMITZ EVERYMAN! BIEDERMANN!

BABETTE Are you – for example – death?

BIEDERMANN Tripe!

BABETTE What else can he be?

BIEDERMANN You must ask: Who are you? He might be Hamlet's ghost. Or the Stone Guest, you know. Or thingumyjig, what's his name: the chap who helped Macbeth . . .

SCHMITZ WHO CALLS ME?

EISENRING Carry on.

SCHMITZ GOTTLIEB BIEDERMANN!

BABETTE You ask him, he's talking to you.

SCHMITZ DO YOU NOT HEAR ME?

BIEDERMANN Who are you, then?

SCHMITZ I AM THE GHOST OF – KNECHTLING.
Babette jumps up and screams.

EISENRING Stop.
He tears the white tablecloth off Schmitz.
You're an idiot! You can't do that. Knechtling! That's impossible. Knechtling was buried today.

SCHMITZ Exactly.
Babette covers her face with her hands.

EISENRING It isn't really him.
He shakes his head over Schmitz.
How can you act in such bad taste?

SCHMITZ That was the only thing I could think of . . .

EISENRING Knechtling! Of all people. An old and faithful collaborator of Herr Biedermann's, just think of

that: buried today – he's still all there, as pale as a tablecloth, white and gleaming like damask, stiff and cold, but to set him up in front of us . . .
He takes Babette by the shoulder:
Word of honour, madam, it isn't really him.
Schmitz wipes away the sweat.

SCHMITZ Sorry.

BIEDERMANN Let's sit down.

ANNA Is that everything now?
They sit down. An embarrassed pause.

BIEDERMANN How about a little cigar, gentlemen?
He offers a box of cigars.

EISENRING Idiot! You can see how Herr Biedermann is trembling . . . Thank you, Herr Biedermann, thank you! . . . If you think that's funny. When you know perfectly well that Knechtling put his head in the gas oven, after our Gottlieb had done all he could for the man. For fourteen years he gave Knechtling work, and that's the thanks –

BIEDERMANN Don't let's talk any more about it.

EISENRING That's your thanks for the goose!
They prepare their cigars.

SCHMITZ Shall I sing something?

EISENRING What?

SCHMITZ 'Goosey, Goosey Gander –'
He sings at the top of his voice:
'Goosey, Goosey Gander, where shall I wander?'

EISENRING That's enough.

SCHMITZ 'Where shall I wander? Upstairs and downstairs –'

EISENRING He's drunk.

SCHMITZ 'And in my lady's chamber – pot.'

EISENRING Don't listen, madam.

SCHMITZ 'Where shall I wander?
Upstairs and downstairs,
And in my lady's chamber – pot!'

BIEDERMANN Chamber-pot, that's funny.

ALL THE MEN 'Goosey, Goosey Gander –'

They make a part song of it, singing sometimes very loud, sometimes very softly, alternating it in every possible way, with laughter and noisy bonhomie. There is a pause, but then it is Biedermann who leads the jollity, till they are all exhausted.

BIEDERMANN Well then – cheers!

They raise their glasses, and sirens are heard in the distance.

What was that?

EISENRING Sirens.

BIEDERMANN Joking apart! –

BABETTE Firebugs! Firebugs!

BIEDERMANN Don't yell.

Babette tears open the window and the sirens come closer, howling to chill the marrow, and race past.

BIEDERMANN At least it's not here.

BABETTE Where can it be?

EISENRING Where the south wind is blowing from.

BIEDERMANN At least it's not here . . .

EISENRING We generally do it like that. We get the fire engine off into some poor district on the outskirts, and later, when the balloon really goes up, they find the way back blocked.

BIEDERMANN No, gentlemen, joking apart –

SCHMITZ But that's how we do it, joking apart.

BIEDERMANN Stop this nonsense, please. Moderation in everything. Can't you see my wife's as white as a sheet?

BABETTE What about you?

BIEDERMANN And anyway, sirens are sirens, I can't laugh about that, gentlemen. Somewhere everything has come to a stop, somewhere the house is on fire, otherwise our fire engine wouldn't be going out.

Eisenring looks at his watch.

EISENRING We must go.

BIEDERMANN Now?

EISENRING I'm afraid so.

SCHMITZ 'Upstairs and downstairs . . .'

Sirens wail again.

BIEDERMANN Make some coffee, Babette!

Babette goes out.

BIEDERMANN And you, Anna, what are you standing there gaping for?

Anna goes out.

Between ourselves, gentlemen, enough is enough. My wife has a weak heart. Let's have no more joking about arson.

SCHMITZ We're not joking, Herr Biedermann.

EISENRING We're firebugs.

BIEDERMANN Gentlemen, quite seriously now –

SCHMITZ Quite seriously.

EISENRING Quite seriously.

SCHMITZ Why don't you believe us?

EISENRING Your house, Herr Biedermann, is very favourably situated, you must admit that: five ignition points like this round the gas-holders, which are unfortunately guarded, and a good south wind blowing –

BIEDERMANN It isn't true.

SCHMITZ Herr Biedermann, if you think we're firebugs, why not say so straight out?

Biedermann looks like a whipped dog.

BIEDERMANN I don't think you're firebugs, gentlemen, it isn't true, you're being unfair to me, I don't think you're – firebugs ...

EISENRING Cross your heart!

BIEDERMANN No! No, no! No.

SCHMITZ Then what do you think we are?

BIEDERMANN My friends ...

They slap him on the back and leave him standing.

Where are you going now?

EISENRING It's time.

BIEDERMANN I swear it, gentlemen, by God!

EISENRING By God?

BIEDERMANN Yes!

He slowly raises his right hand.

SCHMITZ Willie doesn't believe in God any more than you do, Herr Biedermann – you can swear till you're blue in the face.

They walk on towards the door.

BIEDERMANN What can I do to make you believe me?

He stands between them and the door.

EISENRING Gives us matches.

BIEDERMANN Do what?

EISENRING We've none left.

BIEDERMANN You want me to –

EISENRING Yes. If you don't think we're firebugs.

BIEDERMANN Matches?

SCHMITZ As a sign of trust, he means.

Biedermann puts his hand in his pocket.

EISENRING He hesitates. You see? He hesitates.

BIEDERMANN Quiet! – but not in front of my wife . . .

Babette comes back.

BABETTE The coffee will be here in a minute.

Pause.

Do you have to go?

BIEDERMANN Yes, my friends – it's a pity, but there it is – the main thing is that you have come to feel – I don't want to make a song and dance about it, my friend, but why don't we address each other by our first names?

BABETTE H'm.

BIEDERMANN Let's drink to our friendship!

He takes a bottle and the corkscrew.

EISENRING Tell your good husband not to open another bottle on that account, it's not worth it now.

Biedermann uncorks the bottle.

BIEDERMANN Nothing is too much, my friends, nothing is too much, and if there's anything you want – anything at all . . .

He hurriedly fills the glasses and hands them round.

My friends, let's drink!

They clink glasses.
Gottlieb –
He kisses Schmitz on the cheek.

SCHMITZ Joe –
BIEDERMANN Gottlieb.
He kisses Eisenring on the cheek.

EISENRING Willie –
They stand and drink.
All the same, Gottlieb, we have to go now.

SCHMITZ Unfortunately.
EISENRING Madam –
Sirens wail.

BABETTE It was a delightful evening.
Alarm bells ring.

EISENRING Just one more thing, Gottlieb –
BIEDERMANN What is it?
EISENRING You know.
BIEDERMANN If there's anything you want –
EISENRING The matches.
Anna has come in with the coffee.

BABETTE What on earth's the matter?
Out at the back – the sky, Frau Biedermann,
from the kitchen window – the sky is on fire . . .
The light has turned very red as Schmitz and Eisenring bow and leave. Biedermann stands pale and rigid.

BIEDERMANN Thank goodness it isn't here. Thank goodness it
isn't here . . . Thank goodness –
Enter the Doctor of Philosophy.

BIEDERMANN What do you want?
PH.D. I can remain silent no longer.
He takes a document from his breast pocket and reads:
'The undersigned, himself profoundly shocked
by the events now taking place, which even from
our standpoint, it seems to me, can only be char-
acterized as criminal, makes the following de-
claration to the public: –'

Many sirens wail. He reads out a lengthy text of which not a word is intelligible, dogs bark, alarm bells ring, there are shouts and sirens in the distance, the crackling of fire nearby; then he comes up to Biedermann and hands him the document.

I dissociate myself.

BIEDERMANN What of it?

PH.D. I have said what I have to say.
He takes off his glasses and folds them up.

BIEDERMANN Herr Doktor –
The Ph.D. leaves.
Herr Doktor, what am I supposed to do with this?
The Ph.D. steps over the footlights and sits down in the stalls.

BABETTE Gottlieb –

BIEDERMANN He's gone.

BABETTE What was it you gave them? Did I see right? – Were they matches?

BIEDERMANN Why not?

BABETTE Matches?

BIEDERMANN If they were really firebugs, do you think they wouldn't have matches? . . . Babette, Babette, my dear little Babette! *The grandfather clock strikes, the light turns red and as the stage darkens there are heard: alarm bells, the barking of dogs, sirens, the crash of falling timber, hooting, the crackling of fire and cries, until the Chorus moves front stage.*

. . . .

CHORUS There is much that is senseless and nothing
More so than this story:
Which once it had started
Killed many, ah, but not all
And changed nothing.
First explosion.

CHORUS LEADER That was a gas-holder.
Second explosion.

CHORUS What all have foreseen
From the outset,
And yet in the end it takes place,
Is idiocy,
The fire it's too late to extinguish.
Called Fate.
Third explosion.

CHORUS LEADER Another gas-holder.
A series of terrible explosions follows.

CHORUS Woe! Woe! Woe!
Light in the auditorium.

Afterpiece

Characters

HERR BIEDERMANN
BABETTE
ANNA
BEELZEBUB
A FIGURE
A POLICEMAN
A LONG-TAILED MONKEY
WIDOW KNECHTLING

THE CHORUS

The stage has been cleared and is completely empty.
Babette and Biedermann are standing as they were
standing at the end of the previous scene.

BABETTE Gottlieb?

BIEDERMANN Quiet.

BABETTE Are we dead?

A parrot screeches.

What was that?

The parrot screeches.

BIEDERMANN Why didn't you come down before the stairs caught fire? I warned you. Why did you go back into the bedroom?

BABETTE Because of my jewellery.

BIEDERMANN – Of course we're dead!

The parrot screeches.

BABETTE Gottlieb?

BIEDERMANN Quiet now.

BABETTE Where are we now?

BIEDERMANN In heaven. Where else?

A baby cries.

BABETTE What was that?

The baby cries.

To tell you the truth, Gottlieb, this isn't how I pictured heaven –

BIEDERMANN Don't start losing your faith now!

BABETTE Is this how you pictured heaven?

The parrot screeches.

BIEDERMANN That's a parrot.

The parrot screeches.

BABETTE Gottlieb?

BIEDERMANN Don't start losing your faith now!

BABETTE We've been waiting for half an eternity already.

The baby cries.

And there goes that baby again!

The parrot screeches.

Gottlieb?

BIEDERMANN What is it?

BABETTE What's a parrot doing in heaven?

A doorbell rings.

BIEDERMANN Don't keep bothering me, Babette, please. Why shouldn't a parrot go to heaven? If it's done no wrong.

The doorbell rings.

What was that?

BABETTE Our doorbell.

BIEDERMANN Who on earth can it be?

Doorbell, baby and parrot are all heard simultaneously.

BABETTE If only that parrot wasn't here! And that baby! I can't stand it, Gottlieb, a din like that going on for all eternity – it's like a housing estate.

BIEDERMANN Quiet!

BABETTE They can't expect us to put up with that!

BIEDERMANN Calm down.

BABETTE We're not used to that sort of thing.

BIEDERMANN Why shouldn't we be in heaven? All our friends are in heaven, even my solicitor. For the last time, this can't be anything but heaven. What else could it be? It must be heaven. What wrong have we ever done?

The doorbell rings.

BABETTE Shouldn't we open the door?

The doorbell rings.

How did they get hold of our bell?

The doorbell rings.

Perhaps it's an angel . . .

The doorbell rings.

BIEDERMANN I've done no wrong! – I honoured my father and mother, you know that, especially Mother, and that often used to annoy you. All my life I've kept the Ten Commandments, Babette. I've never made myself a graven image, definitely not. I've never stolen; we always had what we needed. And I've never killed. I've never worked on

Sunday. I've never coveted my neighbour's house, or if I did covet it I bought it. I suppose one is allowed to buy! I'm not aware that I tell lies. I haven't committed adultery, Babette, really not – by comparison with other people! . . . You're my witness, Babette, if an angel comes: I had only one fault on earth, I was too kind-hearted, maybe, simply too kind-hearted.

The parrot screeches.

BABETTE Do you understand what it's calling out?

The parrot screeches.

BIEDERMANN Have you killed? I'm only asking. Did you go after other gods? Just that little bit of Yoga! . . . Did you commit adultery, Babette?

BABETTE Who with?

BIEDERMANN Precisely.

The doorbell rings.

We must be in heaven.

Enter Anna in cap and apron.

BABETTE What's Anna doing in heaven?

Anna wanders past; her hair is long and poison-green.

I hope she didn't see you give them the matches, Gottlieb. She's quite capable of reporting it.

BIEDERMANN Matches!

BABETTE I told you they were firebugs, Gottlieb, the very first night –

Enter Anna and a policeman with small white wings.

ANNA I'll call him.

Anna goes out; the angel-policeman waits.

BIEDERMANN You see?

BABETTE What?

BIEDERMANN An angel.

The policeman salutes.

BABETTE I pictured angels differently.

BIEDERMANN We're not living in the Middle Ages.

BABETTE Didn't you picture angels differently?

The policeman turns round and waits.

Shall we kneel?

BIEDERMANN Ask him if this is heaven.

Biedermann encourages the hesitant Babette by nodding his head.

Tell him we've been waiting half an eternity already.

Babette approaches the policeman.

BABETTE My husband and I –

BIEDERMANN Tell him we're victims.

BABETTE My husband and I are victims.

BIEDERMANN Our villa is in ruins.

BABETTE My husband and I –

BIEDERMANN Tell him!

BABETTE – in ruins.

BIEDERMANN He simply can't imagine what we've been through. Tell him! We've lost everything. Tell him! And yet we've done no wrong.

BABETTE You simply can't imagine.

BIEDERMANN What we've been through.

BABETTE All my jewellery was melted!

BIEDERMANN Tell him we've done no wrong –

BABETTE And yet we've done no wrong.

BIEDERMANN – compared with other people!

BABETTE – compared with other people.

The angel-policeman takes out a cigar.

POLICEMAN Have you any matches?

Biedermann turns pale.

BIEDERMANN I? Matches? Why?

A flame as tall as a man blazes up out of the ground.

POLICEMAN I've got a light here, thanks, this will do.

Babette and Biedermann stare at the jet of flame.

BABETTE Gottlieb –

BIEDERMANN Quiet!

BABETTE What's the meaning of that?

Enter a Long-tailed Monkey.

MONKEY What have we here?

POLICEMAN A few damned souls.

The monkey puts on glasses.

BABETTE Gottlieb, we know him, don't we?

BIEDERMANN Who is he?

BABETTE Our Doctor of Philosophy.
The monkey takes the report and leafs through it.

MONKEY How are you all up there?

POLICEMAN Mustn't complain, nobody knows where God lives, but we're all well, mustn't complain – thanks.

MONKEY Why have they been sent to us?
The policeman looks into the report.

POLICEMAN Freethinkers.
The monkey has ten rubber stamps and stamps each time.

MONKEY THOU SHALT HAVE NO OTHER GODS BEFORE ME . . .

POLICEMAN A doctor who gave the wrong injection.

MONKEY THOU SHALT NOT KILL.

POLICEMAN A company director with seven secretaries.

MONKEY THOU SHALT NOT LUST.

POLICEMAN An abortionist.

MONKEY THOU SHALT NOT KILL

POLICEMAN A drunken driver.

MONKEY THOU SHALT NOT KILL.

POLICEMAN Refugees.

MONKEY What was their sin?

POLICEMAN Here: 52 potatoes, 1 umbrella, 2 blankets.

MONKEY THOU SHALT NOT STEAL.

POLICEMAN An income tax adviser.

MONKEY THOU SHALT NOT BEAR FALSE WITNESS . . .

POLICEMAN Another drunken driver.
The monkey stamps without speaking.
Another freethinker.
The monkey stamps without speaking.
Seven partisans. They went to heaven by mistake, and now it turns out that they looted, before they were captured and put against the wall and shot. Looted without uniforms.

MONKEY THOU SHALT NOT STEAL.

POLICEMAN Another abortionist.

MONKEY THOU SHALT NOT KILL.

POLICEMAN And those are the rest.

MONKEY THOU SHALT NOT COMMIT ADULTERY.

> *The monkey stamps at least thirteen reports.*
> Once again nothing but middle-class people! The Devil will be furious. Once again nothing but teenagers! I scarcely dare tell the Devil. Again not a single public figure! Not a single cabinet minister, not a single field-marshal –

POLICEMAN Uhuh.

MONKEY Take the people down below, our Beelzebub has already heated the place, I think, or he's just doing so.

> *The policeman salutes and goes.*

BABETTE Gottlieb – we're in hell!

BIEDERMANN Don't shout!

BABETTE Gottlieb –

> *Babette bursts out sobbing.*

BIEDERMANN Herr Doktor?

MONKEY What can I do for you?

BIEDERMANN It must be a mistake . . . It's quite impossible . . . The situation must be rectified . . . Why are we in hell, my wife and I?

> *To Babette:*
> Compose yourself, Babette, it must be a mistake –
> *To the monkey:*
> Can I speak to the Devil?

BABETTE Gottlieb –

BIEDERMANN Can I speak to the Devil?

> *The monkey gestures into the emptiness, as if there were chairs.*

MONKEY Take a seat.

> *Biedermann and Babette see no chairs.*
> What's the trouble?
> *Biedermann produces documents.*
> What's this?

BIEDERMANN   My driving licence.

MONKEY   We don't need that.
The monkey returns the documents without looking at them.
Your name is Biedermann?

BIEDERMANN   Yes.

MONKEY   Gottlieb Biedermann.

BIEDERMANN   Businessman.

MONKEY   Millionaire.

BIEDERMANN   How do you know?

MONKEY   Of 33 Roseway.

BIEDERMANN   Yes . . .

MONKEY   The Devil knows you.
Babette and Biedermann exchange glances.
Take a seat!
Two fire-blackened chairs come down onto the stage.
Do sit down.

BABETTE   Gottlieb – our chairs!

MONKEY   Do sit down.
Biedermann and Babette sit down.
Do you smoke?

BIEDERMANN   Not any more.

MONKEY   Your own cigars, Herr Biedermann . . .
The monkey takes a cigar.
You were burnt out?

BIEDERMANN   Yes.

MONKEY   Were you surprised?
Seven flames as tall as a man shoot up out of the ground.
I've got matches, thanks.
The monkey lights the cigar and smokes.
To come back to the point, what can I do for you?

BIEDERMANN   We are homeless.

MONKEY   Would you like a slice of bread?

BABETTE   – Bread?

MONKEY   Or a glass of wine?

BIEDERMANN We're homeless!
The monkey calls.

MONKEY Anna!
The monkey smokes.

BABETTE We don't want bread and wine –

MONKEY Don't you?

BABETTE We're not beggars –

BIEDERMANN We're victims.

BABETTE We don't want charity!

BIEDERMANN We aren't used to it.

BABETTE We don't need it!
Enter Anna.

ANNA You called?

MONKEY They don't want charity.

ANNA Very good.
Anna goes.

BIEDERMANN We want our rights.

BABETTE We had a home of our own.

BIEDERMANN Our simple rights.

BABETTE Our simple home.

BIEDERMANN We demand restitution!
The monkey walks away in the manner of a secretary, without a word.

BABETTE What did he mean when he said the Devil knew you?

BIEDERMANN No idea . . .
A grandfather clock strikes.

BABETTE Gottlieb – our grandfather clock!
The grandfather clock has struck nine.

BIEDERMANN We have a claim to everything that was burnt. We were insured. Believe me, I shan't rest until everything has been restored just as it was.
The monkey comes back from the left.

MONKEY One moment. One moment.
The monkey goes out right.

BIEDERMANN The devils are putting on airs!

BABETTE Sh.

BIEDERMANN Well it's true! Next thing we know they'll be

taking finger-prints. As at a consulate. Simply to
give us a guilty conscience.
Babette rests her hand on his arm.
I haven't got a guilty conscience, don't worry, I
shan't get excited, Babette, I shall keep strictly
to the point, strictly to the point.
The parrot screeches.
Strictly to the point!

BABETTE Suppose they ask you about the matches?

BIEDERMANN I gave them. What of it? Everyone gave matches.
Almost everyone. Otherwise the whole city
wouldn't have burnt down. I saw how the fire
blazed up out of every roof. Including the Hof-
manns'! Including Karl's! Including Professor
Mohr's! – Quite apart from the fact that I acted
in good faith!

BABETTE Don't get excited.

BIEDERMANN I ask you, if we, you and I, hadn't given matches,
do you think it would have made any difference
to the disaster?

BABETTE I didn't give any.

BIEDERMANN And anyhow, they can't throw everybody into
hell if everybody did the same thing!

BABETTE Why not?

BIEDERMANN After all, they're bound to show some mercy . . .
The monkey comes back.

MONKEY I'm afraid the Lord of the Underworld isn't here
yet. Unless the lady and gentleman would like to
speak to Beelzebub?

BABETTE Beelzebub?

MONKEY He's here.

BIEDERMANN Beelzebub?

MONKEY But he stinks. You know, he's the one with the
cloven foot and the goat's tail and the horns. You
know him. But he can't help you much, not a poor
devil like Joe.

BIEDERMANN – Joe?
Babette has jumped up.

Sit down!

BABETTE Didn't I tell you straight away, Gottlieb, the very
first night –

BIEDERMANN Keep quiet!

*Biedermann gives Babette a look that makes her
sit down.*

My wife had a weak heart.

MONKEY Oh.

BIEDERMANN My wife was often unable to sleep. Then you hear
ghosts of all kinds. But by daylight, Herr Doktor,
we had no grounds for any suspicion, I swear to
you, not for a second . . .

Babette gives Biedermann a look.

BIEDERMANN Well, I didn't.

BABETTE Then why were you going to throw them out into
the street, Gottlieb, with your own hands and in
the middle of the night?

BIEDERMANN I didn't throw them out!

BABETTE That's just the trouble.

BIEDERMANN And why the devil didn't you throw him out?

BABETTE Me?

BIEDERMANN Instead of giving him breakfast with marmalade
and cheese, you and your soft-boiled eggs, yes,
you!

The monkey smokes the cigar.

In short, Herr Doktor, we had no idea at the time
of what was going on in our house, no idea whatever –

A fanfare of trumpets.

MONKEY That'll be him now.

BABETTE Who?

MONKEY The Lord of the Underworld.

A fanfare of trumpets.

He's been on a visit to heaven and he may be very
bad tempered. We expected him yesterday. There
seems to have been some tough negotiating again.

BIEDERMANN About me?

MONKEY About the last amnesty . . .

The monkey whispers in Biedermann's ear.

BIEDERMANN So I read.

MONKEY What do you say to that?
The monkey whispers in Biedermann's ear.

BIEDERMANN I don't follow you.
The monkey whispers in Biedermann's ear.
How do you mean?
The monkey whispers in Biedermann's ear.
Do you think so?

MONKEY If heaven doesn't keep the Ten Commandments –

BIEDERMANN H'm.

MONKEY Without heaven there can be no hell!

BIEDERMANN H'm.

MONKEY That's what the negotiations are about.

BIEDERMANN About the Ten Commandments?

MONKEY About the principle.

BIEDERMANN H'm.

MONKEY If heaven thinks hell is going to put up with absolutely anything –
The monkey whispers in Biedermann's ear.

BIEDERMANN Strike –!
The monkey whispers in Biedermann's ear.
Do you think so?

MONKEY I don't know, Herr Biedermann, I'm just saying it's possible. Very possible. Depending on the result of these negotiations –
Fanfare of trumpets.
He's coming.
The monkey goes.

BABETTE What did he say?

BIEDERMANN It's possible, he says, very possible, that no one else will be let into hell. From today on. Do you understand: no one at all.

BABETTE Why?

BIEDERMANN Because hell is going on strike.
The doorbell rings.
He says the devils are beside themselves. They

feel cheated, they were hoping for a whole lot of
public figures, and it seems that heaven has par-
doned them. Under these circumstances they re-
fuse to keep hell going any longer. There's talk
of a crisis in hell.

*Anna comes in from the left and goes out from the
right.*

Why is Anna in hell?

BABETTE She stole a pair of stockings from me. I didn't
dare tell you at the time. A new pair of nylon
stockings.

Anna comes in leading Widow Knechtling.

ANNA Take a seat. But if you're Widow Knechtling
you're wasting your time: your husband is a sui-
cide. Take a seat! But you're wasting your
time.

*Anna goes, and Widow Knechtling stands; there is
no chair.*

BABETTE What does she want here?

Biedermann nods to her with sour friendliness.

She means to denounce us, Gottlieb . . .

Babette nods to her with sour friendliness.

BIEDERMANN Let her!

More fanfares, now closer than the first time.

That's nonsense. Damn it all, why didn't Knechtling wait for a week and talk it over with me at a
favourable opportunity? Damn it all, I wasn't to
know that Knechtling would really put his head
in the gas oven, because he'd been given notice . . .

Fanfares closer still.

So I'm not frightened.

Fanfares closer still.

Matches! Matches!

BABETTE Perhaps nobody saw.

BIEDERMANN I won't have all this fuss about a disaster. There
have always been disasters! – And anyhow, just
look at our city! All glass and chrome! To be quite
frank, I must say it's a blessing it was burnt down,

a positive blessing, from a town-planning point
of view –

*Fanfares, then an organ. A gorgeous figure dressed
somewhat, but only somewhat, like a bishop appears
with splendid and solemn bearing. Biedermann and
Babette kneel beside the footlights. The figure stands
in the centre.*

FIGURE   Anna?

The Figure slowly takes off his violet gloves.

I have just come from heaven.

BIEDERMANN   Did you hear?

FIGURE   It's hopeless.

The Figure throws down the first glove.

Anna!

The Figure slowly takes off the other glove.

I doubt whether what I saw was the true heaven;
they said it was, but I doubt it . . . They wear
medals and decorations and there's a smell of in-
cense coming from every loudspeaker. I saw a
Milky Way of decorations, a gala performance that
was enough to make the Devil's blood run cold. I
saw all my clients, all my mass-murderers, and the
little angel's circle round their bald heads; people
greet one another, they wander round drinking
and crying Hallelujah, they giggle over all this
clemency – the saints are strikingly silent, because they are made of stone or wood, gifts on
loan, and the Princes of the Church (I mixed with
the Princes of the Church to find out where God
lives) are also silent, although they are not made
of stone or wood . . .

The Figure throws down the glove.

Anna?

The Figure removes his headgear. It is Eisenring.

I disguised myself. It's the powerful who are up
there and they spend their time pardoning one
another and lo and behold, they didn't recognize
me: – I gave them my blessing.

Enter Anna and the monkey, who bow.
Let me be disrobed!
The Figure, still with splendid bearing, stretches out both arms so that the four silken robes may be unbuttoned, the first silver-white, the second gold, the third violet, the fourth blood-red. The organ falls silent. Biedermann and Babette kneel by the footlights.
Let my tails be brought!

ANNA Very good.

FIGURE And my head-waiter's wig.
They take off the first robe.
I doubt whether it was God who received me. – He knows everything and when he raises his voice he says exactly what is in the newspapers, word for word.
The parrot screeches.
Where is Beelzebub?

MONKEY At the boilers.

FIGURE Let him appear before me.
The light suddenly turns very red.
Why this firelight?

MONKEY He is heating. A few damned souls have just arrived – nobody well known, just the usual smal' fry . . .
They take off the second robe.

FIGURE Tell him to put out the boilers.

MONKEY Put them out?

FIGURE Put them out.
The parrot screeches.
How's my parrot?
The Figure notices Biedermann and Babette.
Ask those people why they're praying.

MONKEY They're not praying.

FIGURE But they're kneeling –

MONKEY They want their home back.

FIGURE They want what?

MONKEY Restitution.

The parrot screeches.

FIGURE I love my parrot. The only living creature that
doesn't change its slogans! I found it once in a
burning house. A faithful bird! I shall set it on
my right shoulder next time I go down to earth.
They take off the third robe.
And now, girlie, my tails!

ANNA Very good.

FIGURE And you, doctor, fetch the bicycles. You remember? The two rusty bicycles.
The monkey and Anna bow and go.

BIEDERMANN Willie! – It is Willie, isn't it? . . . I'm Gottlieb,
your friend – Willie, don't you remember me?
The Figure takes off the fourth and last robe.

BABETTE We've done no wrong, Herr Eisenring. Why have
we been sent to you, Herr Eisenring? We're victims, Herr Eisenring. All my jewellery has been
melted –
The Figure stands in shirt and socks.

BIEDERMANN Why does he pretend not to know us?

BABETTE He feels embarrassed, don't look!
Anna brings the dress trousers.

FIGURE Thanks, girlie, thanks very much.
Anna turns to go.
Anna!

ANNA At your service.

FIGURE Bring two velvet cushions.

ANNA Very good.

FIGURE For the lady and gentleman who are kneeling.

ANNA Very good.
*Anna goes out and the Figure climbs into the dress
trousers.*

BIEDERMANN Willie –

BABETTE You remember us, Herr Eisenring, I'm sure, my
goose was first-class, you said so yourself.

BIEDERMANN Goose and Pommard.

BABETTE With chestnut stuffing.

BIEDERMANN And red cabbage.

BABETTE And candlelight, Herr Eisenring, candlelight!

BIEDERMANN And the way we sang together –

BABETTE Oh yes.

BIEDERMANN Do you really not remember?

BABETTE It was a delightful evening.

BIEDERMANN Forty-nine, Willie, Cave de l'Echannon! The best bottle in my cellar. Willie, didn't I give you everything so that we should be friends?

The Figure flicks specks off the dress trousers.

You're my witness, Babette: Didn't I give everything I had in the house?

BABETTE Even the matches.

Anna brings two red velvet cushions.

Anna takes the cushions to Biedermann and Babette.

ANNA Anything else?

Biedermann and Babette kneel on the red cushions.

FIGURE My waistcoat, girlie, my white waistcoat!

ANNA Very good.

FIGURE And the wig!

Anna goes and the Figure knots his tie.

Cave de l'Echannon –?

Biedermann nods and beams with confidence.

I remember it all, Gottlieb, very clearly, as only the Devil can remember. You clinked glasses and drank to our friendship, and you went so far – it was pretty embarrassing! – as to kiss the Devil's cheek.

The parrot screeches.

BIEDERMANN We didn't know you were devils, Willie. Cross my heart! If we had known you were really devils –

Enter Joe as Beelzebub with a cloven foot, a goat's tail and horns; in addition he is carrying a large coal shovel.

BEELZEBUB What's the matter?

FIGURE Don't bellow.

BEELZEBUB Why are you changing your clothes?

FIGURE We've got to go down to earth again, Joe.

Anna brings the white waistcoat.

Thanks, girlie, thanks very much.
The Figure puts on the waistcoat.
Did you put out the boilers?

BEELZEBUB No.

FIGURE Do as I tell you.
The firelight becomes brighter than before.

BEELZEBUB The coal is in! . . .
Anna brings the jacket.

FIGURE Just a minute, girlie, just a minute!
The Figure buttons up the waistcoat.
I've been in heaven –

BEELZEBUB What happened?

FIGURE I bargained and bargained, I tried everything and
achieved nothing. They won't hand over a single
one. It's hopeless.

BEELZEBUB Not one?

FIGURE Not one.
Anna is holding the jacket.
Doctor!

MONKEY At your service.

FIGURE Call the Fire Brigade.
The monkey bows and goes.

BEELZEBUB They won't hand over a single one!

FIGURE Whoever wears a uniform or did wear a uniform
when he killed, or whoever promises to wear a
uniform when he kills or orders others to kill, is
saved.

BEELZEBUB Saved?

FIGURE Don't bellow.

BEELZEBUB Saved!
The echo is heard from above.

ECHO Saved.

FIGURE Do you hear?

ECHO Saved. Saved. Saved.
Beelzebub gazes upwards.

FIGURE Take your clobber off, Joe, we must go back to
work.
Enter the Chorus.

CHORUS Woe! Woe! Woe!

BABETTE Gottlieb!

BIEDERMANN Quiet!

BABETTE What are they doing here?

CHORUS Good people of our city, see
Us as we helpless stand.
Once the guardians of the city,
Trained to extinguish fires,
Splendidly equipped, oh
Now we are condemned
Forever to stand by and watch
The fires of hell,
Full of goodwill towards the frying citizen,
Helpless.

FIGURE Gentlemen, extinguish hell!
The Chorus is speechless.
I've no intention of running a hell for stuffed shirts and intellectuals, pickpockets, adulterers, servants who have stolen nylon stockings, and conscientious objectors – I shouldn't dream of it!
The Chorus is speechless.
What are you waiting for?

CHORUS Ready are we.
Carefully coiled are the hoses
In accordance with regulations,
Polished and carefully greased and of brass
Is each windlass.
Everyone knows what his task is,
Polished too and carefully tested,
To make sure that we have full pressure,
Is our pump,
Likewise of brass.

CHORUS LEADER And the hydrants?

CHORUS Everyone knows what his task is.

CHORUS LEADER We are ready. –
The Figure straightens his dress-suit.

FIGURE Go ahead.

The firelight has become very bright again.

CHORUS LEADER Man the hoses!

Man the pump!

Man the ladders!

The firemen run to their places and shout:

CHORUS Ready.

CHORUS LEADER We are ready.

FIGURE Go ahead.

The hissing of hydrants; the firelight dies down.

MONKEY Well, Herr Biedermann, it's as I foresaw –

FIGURE Doctor!

MONKEY Yes, sir?

FIGURE Our bicycles!

MONKEY Very good.

FIGURE And my wig, girlie, my wig!

ANNA Very good.

FIGURE And my parrot!

The monkey and Anna go.

BEELZEBUB My childhood faith! My childhood faith!

Thou shalt not kill, ha, and I believed it.

What are they making of my childhood faith!

The Figure cleans his finger nails.

I, the son of a charcoal burner and a gypsy woman, who couldn't read but knew the Ten Commandments off by heart, I'm possessed by the Devil. Why? Simply because I scorned all commandments. Go to hell, Joe, you're possessed by the Devil, everyone said to me, and I went to hell. I lied, because then everything went better, and I became possessed by the Devil. I stole whatever took my fancy and became possessed by the Devil. I whored with whatever came my way, married or unmarried, because I had the urge to, and I felt fine when I gave way to my urge, and became possessed by the Devil.

And they feared me in every village, for I was stronger than all of them, because I was possessed by the Devil. I tripped them up on their

way to church, because I felt the urge, I set fire
to their stables while they were praying and singing, every Sunday, because I felt the urge, and I
laughed at their God who did not lay hold of me.
Who felled the fir tree that killed my father in
broad daylight? And my mother, who prayed for
me, died of worry over me, and I entered the
orphanage to set fire to it, and the circus to set
fire to it, because I felt the urge more and more,
and I started fires in every town simply in order
to be possessed by the Devil. – Thou shalt!
Thou shalt not! Thou shalt! Because we had no
newspapers and no radio out there in the forest,
we had only a Bible, and therefore I believed that
one became possessed by the Devil if one killed
and ravished and murdered and mocked every
commandment and destroyed whole cities – that's
what I believed! . . .

The Figure laughs.

It's no laughing matter, Willie!

Anna brings the wig.

FIGURE Thanks, girlie, thanks very much.

The monkey brings two rusty bicycles.

BEELZEBUB It's no laughing matter. I feel like vomiting when
I see the way things are going. What are they
making of my childhood faith! I can't eat as much
as I want to vomit.

The Figure has put on the wig.

FIGURE Get ready!

The Figure takes a rusty bicycle.

I'm burning to see my old customers again, the
fine people who never come to hell, I'm burning
to serve them afresh! . . . Once again sparks and
crackling flames, sirens that are always too late,
the barking of dogs and smoke and human cries
– and ashes!

Beelzebub unbuckles his goat's tail.

Are you ready?

BEELZEBUB One moment –
The Figure swings himself up onto the saddle and rings the bell.
I'm just coming.
Beelzebub unbuckles his cloven foot.

CHORUS LEADER Stop pump!
Down hoses!
Off water!
The red firelight disappears completely.

FIGURE Ready?
Beelzebub takes the other bicycle.
Beelzebub swings himself up onto the saddle and rings the bell.
What about your horns?
Beelzebub has to stop and take off his horns.
Anna?

ANNA Yes, sir?

FIGURE Yes, sir?

FIGURE Thanks, girlie, thanks very much for all your services. Why are you so glum all day long? I've only seen you laugh once. Do you remember – when we sang the song about Goosey, Goosey Gander and the chamber-pot?
Anna laughs.
We'll sing it again!

ANNA Oh please!
Enter the Chorus.

CHORUS Good people of our city, see –

FIGURE Keep it short!

CHORUS – hell is extinguished.

FIGURE Thank you. –
The Figure puts his hand in his trouser pocket.
Have you any matches?

BEELZEBUB Not me.

FIGURE Nor me.

BEELZEBUB It's always the same!

FIGURE People will give us some . . .
The monkey brings the parrot.

My parrot!
The Figure places the parrot on his right shoulder.
Before I forget, doctor: we're not accepting any
more souls here. Tell the good people hell is on
strike. And if an angel comes to look for us, say
we're on earth.
Beelzebub rings his bell.
Off we go.
Schmitz and Eisenring cycle off, waving.

BOTH So long, Gottlieb, all the best!
The Chorus comes to the front of the stage.

CHORUS Beams of the sun,
Lashes of the eye divine,
Day is once more breaking –

CHORUS LEADER Over the resurrected city.

CHORUS Hallelujah!
The parrot screeches in the distance.

BABETTE Gottlieb?

BIEDERMANN Quiet now.

BABETTE Are we saved?

BIEDERMANN Don't start losing your faith now.
Widow Knechtling goes.

CHORUS Hallelujah!

BABETTE Frau Knechtling has gone.

CHORUS Finer than ever,
Risen again from rubble and ashes
Is our city,
Cleared away without trace and forgotten
The rubble,
Forgotten too
Those who were burnt to a cinder
And their cries from the flames –

BIEDERMANN Life goes on.

CHORUS History they have become
And are silent.

CHORUS LEADER Hallelujah!

CHORUS Finer than ever,
Richer than ever,